CHILD-CARE

HOW TO LOOK AFTER YOUR GRANDCHILDREN AND MAKE IT FUN!

Sheila Marlin and Dr Lis Paice

BLOOMSBURY

Published 2013 by Featherstone, an imprint of Bloomsbury Publishing plc
50 Bedford Square, London, WC1B 3DP www.bloomsbury.com

ISBN 978-1-4081-9345-7

Text © Dr Lis Paice and Sheila Marlin 2013
Design © Lynda Murray
Cover illustration © Lisa Hunt
Photogaphs © Shutterstock

Acknowledgments

We are grateful to our families, co-grandparents and other friends for sharing their experiences and perspectives. We thank Drs Caroline Fertleman, Ramesh Mehta, Sue Morrison and Kate Jolowicz for their helpful comments on the chapters about sickness and accidents. Above all, we are grateful to our grandchildren for being such fun to look after and such good friends as they grow up.

Printed in Great Britain by Latimer Trend & Company Limited

10 9 8 7 6 5 4 3 2 1

This book is produced using paper that is made from wood grown in managed, sustainable forests. It is natural, renewable and recyclable. The logging and manufacturing processes conform to the environmental regulations of the country of origin.

To see our full range of titles visit www.bloomsbury.com

Contents

Introduction

The idea for this book came to us when chatting to other grandparents about the childcare responsibilities that we all seemed to be taking on. For most of us it came as a surprise that our children would look to us for help with regular childcare, as opposed to occasional babysitting or emergency cover for a sick child. But as more and more women return to work after maternity leave, and as the cost of professional childcare continues to escalate, it clearly makes sense for parents to look to their own parents for help, and they are doing just that in droves!

The trouble is, most grandparents have pretty full lives already. Your first grandchild is likely to appear when you are years away from retirement and with your own parents still alive and in need of support. It may be easier in that situation to offer financial rather than personal help, though many grandparents do reduce their own working hours to take on the care of their grandchildren. Other anxieties flit across your mind. What will the impact be on your own relationships, your retirement plans? Can you remember how to do it? Will it be too exhausting? And, most worrying of all, what if something were to happen to the child while in your care?

Every grandparenting relationship will be different, even within the same family. How much time you can spare and how much you can manage physically will change over time. What you are able to do with the latest addition may be very different from what you did for the first. Different families will have different views on your role. In our experience, the most common pattern seems to be for grandparents to undertake between ten and 16 hours a week, looking after one or two children, sharing the care with a day nursery or childminder. That sort of commitment brings significant responsibilities for supporting the children's development as well as for keeping them safe, warm and fed.

In writing this book together, we have used our own experience of being closely involved with the care of our grandchildren, and the experiences of friends and family. Sheila has brought in her expertise as a Montessori teacher, and Lis has drawn on her training and networks as a physician – though not a paediatrician or GP. We have used anecdotal stories to make a point wherever possible. With many of the issues we raise, there is no right or wrong answer, and a story makes it clear this is just the way things panned out for these particular people. The stories all have their basis in real life but we have changed the names and any identifying details to avoid compromising our friends and family. We found a number of very helpful websites, which we have referred to in the text and listed again at the end of the book, along with a short list of books we found especially useful.

Children are individuals with different passions and different ways of developing. Some of the suggestions in this book will work better for your grandchildren than others. They have all worked well for at least some of the grandchildren we have cared for. As sisters, our own attitudes were influenced by memories of our maternal grandmother, who lived with us. She was Dutch and taught us her language and customs. She was one of Maria Montessori's first students, and we can still remember sorting out the coloured silks and playing with the beads and other bits of special equipment she brought with her from Holland. Her philosophy of respecting and encouraging independence in the child pervaded our house and her sitting room was a haven of love and peace where we always felt welcome.

Parents trust grandparents to love their children and keep them safe. They also trust us to provide their children with the opportunities to develop physical, intellectual and social skills. We hope that this book will help you do all this without giving up your life, damaging your health or emptying your bank account, and that you will have as much fun looking after your grandchildren as we have had with ours.

The family were round at Granny's for Sunday lunch, and the grown-ups were sitting chatting over coffee. Three-year-old Harry was looking thoughtful, 'Am I coming here tomorrow as well?' he asked his mother.

'Yes, dear, just like every Monday.'

'And will you and Dad be coming too?'

'No, I am so sorry darling but we just can't, we have to go to work.'

'Yay!!' shouted the unfeeling child, jumping up and down.
'I NEED my Granny days!'

Your first grandchild

Holding that impossibly tiny bundle that is your first grandchild for the first time can be a powerful experience. We are hard-wired by evolution to be fiercely protective of our children's children and that initial rush of emotion is part of how it works.

New roles

Becoming a grandparent can be something you have longed for with vicarious broodiness. Or it may come as a shock, before you are ready for it in terms of either self-image or responsibilities. One thing is for sure, and that is that your relationship with your children undergoes an immediate change. They take a giant step forward into centre stage in the role of 'parent'; your role is to take a step back and yield that space.

It would be unusual if you didn't feel a bit ambivalent about all this. You have lots of experience to share and help to offer, but the parents might well have done their own reading and talking to friends with babies. They will probably have discussed everything from breastfeeding to baby-led weaning, and from slings to transport systems. They may feel that you will not understand or approve of some of the decisions they are making together, and might therefore be wary of discussing everything with you.

Don't be surprised if you are not asked to do much, or even to visit much, at this early stage. Fathers these days often take paternity leave to help the new mother and bond with the baby. This is a special time for a young couple, and it is common for them to be quite protective of it.

Waiting in the wings

The best opportunity for serious grandparental input comes when paternity leave is over and the new mother is on her own with the baby during the day for the first time. It makes sense to discuss whether and when the mother would like you around, and to plan ahead accordingly, booking annual leave or cancelling commitments, so that you can start when the father goes back to work. Even if you were never that great with babies, just visiting, making a meal, getting the shopping in, and providing some adult conversation can make a huge difference. If early offers of help are rejected, keep the door open, as even the most confident new mother can become overwhelmed in time.

If the mother doesn't have a partner and needs more support than you can provide yourself, there are other sources of help. A doula, for example, will support her through the birth and during the early post-natal weeks. Or she could book a maternity nurse for a few weeks (particularly helpful if the mother has had a caesarean section and can't lift or drive).

Earl had not been a 'new man' with his own children, but when his daughter asked for his help with her new baby he was prepared to do what he could. He took the baby out for hour-long walks and turned out to be a champion baby-soother, giving his daughter a few hours to herself each day to catch up on sleep or do some chores.

Co-grandparents

The arrival of the new baby is an opportunity to connect with the other set of grandparents. You now have a new interest in common with them, and you may be able to share grandparenting duties in times to come, especially in providing cover for emergencies. You could start by sending them your photos of the new arrival as a good opening and if you can add a message about how great a parent their child is proving to be, so much the better. Don't let yourself feel competitive about who helps more or is better with babies. There will be enough opportunities for childcare to satisfy everyone.

> When Daisy was born, her mother had a bad case of post-natal depression and could not look after her for the first few months. When her husband had to go back to work, he hired a baby nurse to care for Daisy during the day. The two grandmothers, who also had full-time jobs, took turns with him at covering the nights until Daisy was able to sleep through and her mother got better.

Advice, criticism and interference

Soothing a baby is a bit like riding a bike: once learned the reflexes are never forgotten. So you will probably find that the new baby calms down more quickly in your arms than in those of his parents. This discovery isn't quite as gratifying for the parents as it is for you, and it is important not to make them feel inadequate as you demonstrate your baby-whispering skills!

The really big rule for grandparents, at this stage and later, is to be very careful about offering advice, and to avoid anything that smacks of criticism or interference. Advice that has been asked for can be a very welcome support; unsolicited advice is a burden and an irritation. If it cuts across what the doctor or health visitor has advised, it can be a worry. If your child's partner doesn't agree with your advice, you may be the unwitting source of strife. And if you are wrong, you will not be readily forgiven. If the parents ask for advice, by all means give them the benefit of your experience, but don't push your theories or go beyond the specific question you were asked. If they reject your advice, let it go.

> It is more blessed to give than to receive – especially if the gift is advice!

At times, it can be really hard to bite your tongue, but try your best. Respect the resourcefulness and good sense of the parents and allow them to learn by their own mistakes. If there is something you really feel you must say, in the interests of your grandchild's health or safety, talk to someone you trust first, to make sure you are not blowing the issue out of proportion. If you decide to go ahead, choose your time carefully, ask the parents' permission to say what is on your mind, and then say your piece calmly, rationally and without allocating blame.

How can I help?

The chances are that, somewhere between three months and one year, the mother will need to go back to work. You may be yearning to spend as much time as possible with the 'little darling' and happy to drop everything else to do it. Or you may feel that, as far as childcare is concerned, you have been there, done that, and got the stained T-shirt! Whichever, as a grandparent you usually have choices, as do the parents. You need to talk about what they want and what you can offer.

Emergencies

The parents' annual leave will quickly run out if they have to take time off work whenever the child gets a fever and can't go to nursery. Even if you are working full-time and can't offer regular care, you may want to help out in emergencies. Keep some of your annual leave in reserve for this purpose, and make sure you get to know the child well enough to be accepted as a carer when he is feeling ill.

Susan had her own busy life in the week, but was happy to devote her weekends to the grandchildren. They were in two families, living two hours or so away by train, in opposite directions. She visited each family on alternate weekends. She would arrive on Saturday afternoon, have fun with the children and chat to the parents, babysit while the parents had their fortnightly evening out, stay over for Sunday lunch, and be back home by Sunday afternoon.

Carol's daughter Wendy had a high-powered job to go back to after her maternity leave and she arranged a place for her baby daughter in a long-day nursery. Wendy explained that reliability was crucial to keeping her job. 'Nurseries never get sick and they don't go on holiday,' was how she put it. Carol understood but pointed out that babies do get sick, and she was very willing to step in should that happen. She suggested that she do the nursery pick-up once a week, getting there a bit earlier than Wendy usually did and having some time to play with her grandchild before Wendy came home. When the baby did get ill and had to be kept at home for a week, it made all the difference that Carol could step in as a familiar figure and look after her.

Regular day-care

Taking on regular responsibility for childcare during the week is only possible if you are not working yourself or are working part-time. Some grandparents manage five days a week, but it is more usual for grandparents to share care with a nursery or childminder. The advantage of doing it this way is that childcare does not totally take over your life. The child gains from socialising with other children some days and having your undivided attention on others. And it is a huge financial help to the parents not to have to pay for care every day of the week.

Agreeing to do set days a week is a heavy responsibility so don't promise more than you can realistically do because reliability is paramount. If there are days when you know you won't be able to make it, flag them up weeks ahead so that other arrangements can be made. Remember, it won't be too long before your grandchildren are disappearing off to school, so don't abandon all your own interests and friends.

Weekends and holidays

If you don't live close enough to offer regular day-care, you may be able to have your grandchild to stay, for weekends or longer. These arrangements bring their own challenges as the child may be more anxious about being away from home when it involves sleeping over. A happy day full of excitement and fun may end in wails of homesickness at bedtime. Make sure she brings a few of her favourite bedtime toys and books, and that you know her bedtime ritual in full detail. A bedtime phone call with the parents is a big help for some children, and planning this in advance avoids disappointment – on either side.

Bill and Selina were worried about how Jeevan would be settling in on his first night away from home, so decided to call to wish him goodnight. Unfortunately they had not said they would call or agreed a time. When Jeevan came to the phone he was dismissive. 'I can't talk right now,' he told them importantly. 'I'm too busy having hot chocolate!'

Live-in grandparenting

Moving into the family's home, or having them move into yours, may be one of the options under consideration. You may find it an appealing idea if you are on your own and get on well with both the parents. It is a huge decision to take though, and one that will change your life irrevocably. Factors to consider are what opportunities you will have to make your own friends and build a new life if you move away from your own home. What are the parents' expectations of your contribution financially and in terms of housework or childcare? What will your status be when the grandchildren grow up?

Dorothy was 70 when her husband died. Her son Charles and his wife Ellen asked her to live with them and their two, soon to be three, children. They were going to have to move anyway to accommodate the new arrival and it would be a great help to have Dorothy in the house when Ellen went back to work. After mulling the invitation over, Dorothy came back with certain conditions. She would move in provided she had her own kitchen, bathroom, sitting room and bedroom. She would look after the older children after school and was happy to babysit in the evenings, but she could not cope with a baby by day. She would get her own meals and the children's tea, but the house would have to be within walking distance of a shop. Charles was taken aback at this list of conditions, but Ellen saw the sense. They finally found an old house that met all the requirements. Dorothy became the heart of the home, always there for the children when the parents were at work, but tactfully withdrawing on their return. She lived with the family until her death 15 years later, and enjoyed being an important part of the family to the very end.

Grandparenting from afar

These days living far away doesn't have to mean foregoing a relationship with your grandchildren. Air travel is not as expensive as it was, especially out of season. When you do visit, don't be surprised if the children are shy and cling to their parents. Give them some time to get reacquainted before you sweep them up in your arms for a big hug. Even better is to keep in regular touch with them from the start, through Skype and email, telephone and letters, so that your visits are part of a continuous process of engagement. Research by the Daycare Trust (**www.daycaretrust.org.uk**) showed that there is a growing trend for grandparents who live far away to be flown in to help with childcare in emergencies, or to cover busy periods at the parents' work.

Rachel's memory of having long-distance grandparents herself was that telephone calls from Turkey were prohibitively expensive. Communication was by letters and photos. 'Care packages' arrived periodically, containing delicacies such as dried apricots, jams, and cheeses, but she had no direct relationship with her grandparents until they moved to the UK, leaving another set of grandchildren back home, bereft.

In contrast, ease of air travel today means Rachel and her husband visit their Australian grandchildren at least once a year. Telephoning and emailing of photos and videos goes on all the time. The grandchildren, age one and three, are adept at communicating by Skype. They chat away, hold things up to the camera for their grandparents to see, and have a special ritual for kissing goodbye at the end of the calls. When Rachel and her husband arrive for a visit, the children pitch themselves into their arms with joyous recognition.

Krishna's little Canadian grandsons have been to his home for a visit and since then Krishna has taken to writing them simple stories based on photographs of places and things they know from their stay. He emails the photos for the parents to print off and then tells the story to them over Skype, while they examine the pictures. He also took out a subscription to a children's magazine that he sends on to them with little comments and special messages in the margins.

Step-grandparenting

You may find yourself becoming a step-grandparent, an honorary grandparent, or the grandparent of a child adopted at an older age. Be ready to welcome your new grandchild with the same loving generosity as you show your other grandchildren, but let the child set the pace. He may have a good relationship with his birth grandparents and not want any more. Let him choose what he calls you. Naturally you won't feel the same connection with him at first, and he may be shy or hostile with you, but your love and interest will develop as you get to know him. At the very least, buy him the same kind of birthday and Christmas presents, be as willing to babysit or provide emergency cover for him, and include him in holiday plans. The parents will appreciate your fair and even-handed approach, and you may be surprised at how your new grandchild responds in time.

Being a parent to your grandchildren

Teenage pregnancy, or parental death, ill-health or disappearance may leave you acting as the parent to your grandchildren. This is really tough and you will need all your reserves of courage, strength and patience. Care given by loving grandparents can help children cope with trauma and tragedy, but don't underestimate the toll it will take on your own health and resources. Make sure you tap into all possible sources of support and don't be reluctant to ask for help, including from the other relatives of your grandchildren. The websites **www.grandparentsasparents. org.uk** and **www.grandparents-association. org.uk** have useful information about your rights, legal issues and what help is available.

When Helena's daughter remarried, her new husband already had four children of his own. Helena extended a welcome to them all, but the two teenagers were angry with their father and not interested in new relatives.

The younger two were also disturbed at their parents splitting up, but they enjoyed playing with their new step-siblings and were soon calling Helena 'Grandma' like all the others.

Reaching an agreement

When agreeing to undertake childcare on a regular basis, there are some practical details to sort out with the parents. It may feel awkward to take a business-like approach to who will do what, and who will provide what, and who will pay for what, but if you can bear to do it, you will avoid unfortunate misunderstandings. You don't want to overstep boundaries, or disappoint expectations but nor do you want to feel taken for granted or exploited.

The costs involved in taking on childcare are substantial. If this is really not of any concern to you, and you are happy to pay for everything that comes along, saying so straight out will be very helpful to the young couple who may be worrying how to broach the issue.

In the more realistic scenario where you are happy to bear some costs, but feel the parents should pay for others, you will need to talk.

Here are some things you should sit down and talk through with the parents at the start and again from time to time when the situation changes. Make a list of what matters to you which could include any of the following:

1. Where will the childcare take place?

2. How many days a week will you care for the child? For how many hours each day? How flexible can they and you be?

3. How will the child get to you, or how will you get to the parents' home?

4. What equipment will you need if it is at yours (highchair, cot, pushchair), and who will provide it?

5. What supplies will be required (nappies, wipes, changes of clothes, rain gear) and who will provide them?

6. What meals will you be providing? What views do they have about what you offer the child? Is there anything you should not give? If you are caring in their home, who will do the shopping for food?

7. What are their views on disciplinary methods and boundaries?

8. If in their home, are there any other tasks they are expecting you to do? (Don't volunteer to do the housework, your hands will be full enough.)

9. Are they happy for you to give a dose of paracetamol or ibuprofen should the child be unwell, or would they prefer you to ring them first?

10. Whom should you call in an emergency? How can you reach them?

11. How do they feel about you sharing your cultural heritage or your beliefs with the child?

12. What are their holiday plans? Can they let you know in good time?

13. Can they find cover for times when you will be away or ill yourself? How much notice do they need?

14. Are they following any particular child-rearing book, and if so, can you borrow it?

Transitions

Whatever pattern of childcare you decide to offer, it will change over time: brothers and sisters arrive, your other children start families and want help, the older grandchildren start school, parents may split up, remarry, step-grandchildren appear, the parents' economic situation changes, for better or worse. Your own life changes too as your parents become more dependant or die, you take on a new role at work or in the community, or you retire. Your health or that of your partner may fail. Some of these changes are predictable, many are not. Be prepared for things to change and be aware that you might feel stressed and uncertain all over again when they do. As more grandchildren appear, you may find your enthusiasm for going through it all yet again wanes. But for each child their relationship with you will be new and special. Try to keep up the same standard of involvement as you did with the older ones, provided health and geography allow. It is only fair, and it may turn out that your youngest grandchild is the one that becomes the most loyal friend in your old age.

Making your home safe

Many grandparents say that the biggest source of stress they have about looking after the children is that something bad will happen while they are in charge. In fact, children are as safe with their grandparents as with anyone, but it is true that accidents around the home are the most common cause of death for under-fives, and most of them are predictable and preventable. For your own peace of mind, make sure you have done what you can to reduce the risks, especially if you are going to be caring for the child in your own home.

Make your home safe

Safety on stairs

Falling down stairs is one of the commonest childhood accidents. From the time that your grandchild starts to crawl to the time he can manage the stairs reliably and safely on his own, you will need a stairgate at the bottom and top of the stairs.

Be slow to take the stair gates down if you have more than one child to look after and they play upstairs. Many is the child who has been pushed down the stairs by a younger sibling!

Debbie looked after her grandson Matthew in her home once a week. He was at the crawling stage, but as he had shown no interest in learning to climb the stairs, and she was with him non-stop all day, she had not put up safety gates. One day a delivery arrived. By the time she had signed for it and taken it in, Matthew had disappeared. She ran frantically from room to room looking for him until she heard a crowing noise from the top of the stairs and saw Matthew's little face looking down at her triumphantly.

Stairs can be dangerous for you too. It is hard to see the steps when you are carrying a baby or small child, especially when you are going downstairs, and it is easy to miss your footing. Keep one hand free for the banister, putting anything else you must carry in pockets or in a bag over your shoulder and avoid wearing backless shoes or slippers.

Avoiding falls

Falls are one of the commonest causes of
injury in children. Babies regularly get hurt
rolling off sofas and beds (the first time you
discover they can roll over will be the one
time you take a chance), wriggling out of
highchairs, and overturning baby walkers.
Identify somewhere safe where you can put
the child when you need to answer the door
or go to the toilet.

Toddlers love to climb. An adventurous
toddler is strong enough to pull a small table
or chair into place to climb onto a kitchen
counter or a window sill, but is too young to
see the dangers in doing so. Toddlers can't be
trusted not to climb out of an open window or
over the rail of a balcony. Lock any accessible
window shut or get a special window lock that
will limit how far it can open (and hang the
key close by, so you can find it when you need
to open the window fully).

Kitchen caution

Kitchens are a magnet for crawlers and
toddlers when you are cooking. If you
are on your own, restrain the child in a
highchair, or sit them at the kitchen table
with something to do. 'No running around
in the kitchen!' is the rule.

If you and your grandchild enjoy cooking
and like to spend time in the kitchen, you
might consider buying a kitchen safety
stand - an enclosed box that a child of
walking age can stand in without danger
of falling. There is even a highchair that
can be turned into one of these, or into a
low table and chair, as required:
http://www.littlehelper.

Get back in the habit of turning saucepan
handles away from the edge of the cooker,
make sure there are no trailing cords and
keep children away from the oven. The
kitchen has plenty of other hazards for
small children, so keep them out when
you are not there, perhaps by putting a
stairgate at the entrance.

Living-room

Unless you have an exceptionally roomy home, the chances are that your living-room will become the children's playroom when they are with you. Look at it with a child's eyes. Anything bright and shiny will be an attraction, from the television remote to the ornaments on the coffee table. Look out for anything that can be pulled down on top of them, knocked over, broken, swallowed, or tripped on. Your grandchild will want to explore and you do not want to be always saying no.

If you like to take your hot drink into the living-room, establish a safe place for you to put it where it can't be reached or knocked over. Don't try to drink it with the child on your lap. Scalds from cups of tea or coffee are one of the commonest injuries to babies and children, and their skin is so delicate that the drink doesn't have to be straight from the kettle to cause harm.

Bathroom safety

Take a look at your bathroom as another potential source of danger. Make sure cleaning products and medicines are stored where a child can't see or reach them. If giving the child a bath is to be part of your responsibilities, remember about running the cold in first and testing the temperature. Water straight from the hot tap can be hot enough to scald a child. Never leave a child unsupervised in a bathroom when there is water in the bath. They may climb in and a small child can drown in just a few centimetres of water. There are various kinds of bath seats now available for babies to help them to sit up and splash about in the bath, but they don't make it any safer for you to leave them, even for a moment.

Medicines

Grandparents' medicines are a well-known risk. We are more likely to be taking pills and tablets and less likely to have established a place to store them in our homes out of reach of children. Child-resistant containers and individual packs do slow toddlers down, but by the age of three most children will be able to open them within seconds. Children will swallow medicines if they get hold of them, even when you might think them old enough to know better. The only really safe thing to do is to keep all medicines out of their sight and reach. Be careful not to let any pills drop on the floor and roll out of sight.

Pierre was cleaning the bath when his baby granddaughter crawled in to watch. He turned to pick her up and found she was examining a large grey capsule she had discovered under the sink. He recognized one of his wife's chemotherapy medicines, which must have fallen on the floor when she was counting out her pills for the day. The capsule was fortunately still intact, and a careful count showed that no others were missing, but the episode was a shock and a wake-up call to both grandparents.

Handbags

'Granny's bag' has been identified by paediatricians as a particular safety risk for children, and not surprisingly. For a child, an adult's handbag is a repository of delights with things like keys, mobile phones and sweets inside. The urge to explore further is strong and if she finds pills or tablets, she will probably eat them. Even loose change is a hazard - coins are responsible for nearly 20% of swallowing or choking-related visits to emergency departments. The message is simple: hang your handbag out of reach!

Everyday poisons

The urge for children to put things in their mouths is very strong, even when the taste might be vile. Children are rushed to hospital every day having drunk cleaning fluids or bitten into washing machine capsules or eaten dishwasher tablets or swallowed slug pellets. Toddlers are hard-wired to explore. Given a chance, they will empty your shopping bags, pull open your kitchen drawers and rummage in your cupboards. Don't rely on your grandchildren having the sense not to try unknown liquids or items. Keep all household poisons high out of reach or fit safety latches to your kitchen and bathroom cupboards.

Your grandchild and your pet

If you have a pet cat or dog you will need to consider how to minimise any risk they may pose to your grandchild. Children and pet dogs or cats often become great friends, with the pet putting up with a bit of rough and tumble and walking away when they have had enough. Nonetheless, there are potential risks to be managed, especially with babies. A small being that waves its arms and mews may awake the natural hunting instincts in a dog. A crying baby may irritate it. Pets can be jealous of attention paid to a child or resentful if admonished for wanting attention themselves. If you have a pet and you are taking on childcare, there is useful advice on how to deal with these issues on several websites, such as
http://www.doggonesafe.com/baby_safety_around_dogs
and
http://www.safekids.co.uk/catsandbabiesorchildren.html

Garden safety

Ensure your garden is a safe environment for your grandchildren to explore, free of broken glass or boards with nails sticking out. Lock the garden shed and clear away pet faeces from the grass. If you get the paddling pool out, empty it at the end of the supervised session. If you have a garden pond, the Royal Society for the Prevention of Accidents (RoSPA) recommends filling it in until the children are at least six. If that seems too much to ask, put a fence around it, or install a safety mesh. In the UK, every year, five or six children under the age of six drown in garden ponds, often when visiting homes other than their own. Most of the drownings involved toddlers and the supervising adult was usually quite close by but momentarily distracted. For more information have a look at the RoSPA fact sheet: **www.rospa.com/leisuresafety/default.aspx**

Make sure the child can't make his way into a neighbour's garden where all these hazards may be present. Some children are born rovers and as soon as they can move they are intent on seeing the world. Make sure they can't wander off on your watch.

Peter was a little boy with an impulse to roam. His grandfather fixed up a childproof latch on the garden gate, but one day he must have managed to climb right over the gate, because it was shut but he had gone. Fortunately he was found safe and sound, four streets away.

Wheels

Children love riding on anything with wheels. A scooter, tricycle or a small bike with stabilisers will provide lots of fun in the garden, but make sure the child wears a helmet when riding on a hard surface. Scooters can go really fast, especially on a slope, and collisions are common. Don't let your grandchildren scoot or pedal on public pavements unless you are absolutely sure that they can control the vehicle and that you can control them. If you are thinking of buying something with wheels for your grandchild, discuss it with the parents first – they may have strong views about what and when – and be prepared to buy the relevant safety gear at the same time.

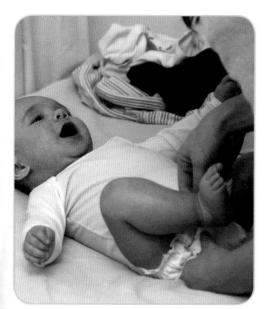

Choking hazards

Of course you know all about keeping anything small enough to disappear into a baby's mouth well away from him. Buttons, beads, marbles, deflated balloons and bits of Lego are a particular danger. Nappy bags are the latest hazard along those lines. Small, scented and stored next to the changing surface, they are easily grabbed and sucked into babies' mouths to cause choking, just the way a bit of popped balloon would do. Keep them, and all other kinds of plastic bags, well out of reach.

Choking on food

Nearly half the cases of choking seen in emergency departments are caused by foods. Grapes, cherry tomatoes, rounds of raw carrot, chunks of hotdog or other meat, jelly cubes and sweets are all of a perfect size to block the main airway if inhaled rather than swallowed. Peanuts are notorious for going down a bit further and blocking a smaller airway, where they set up an inflammatory reaction. Until your grandchild can be trusted to chew these foods properly, it makes sense to cut them up or in the case of the less healthy options, just avoid them altogether. Choking is much more likely to happen if the child is distracted while eating, so don't allow eating on the move, and depress any horseplay or excessive hilarity at your table.

Strings and cords

Toddlers can get into trouble by wrapping strings or cords round their necks, especially when no-one is watching them, so don't tie toys to the cot and clip the cords of bedroom blinds or curtains up where your grandchild can't reach. Position the cot where the child can't reach out and grab anything.

For more advice and information about safety at home have a look at these websites:

www.safekids.co.uk/ AroundtheHomeCategory.html and **www.rospa.com/childsafety**

Delegation

As a rule, the higher the ratio of responsible adults to children, the safer the child will be. If you have a partner to share the childcare with, everything will be much easier. If not, you may have a friend who would enjoy joining you from time to time. If you do, don't lose sight of your responsibility. You can't leave your grandchild even briefly in the care of someone the parents don't know and haven't agreed to as a carer: they have entrusted their child to you, not your friend.

First aid training

You are the child's most important safety feature. When you are with her and paying attention she is unlikely to come to harm. However, even with the best of care and attention, accidents and emergencies do happen. When they do, your ability to stay calm and cope can make all the difference. As well as preparing a safe environment for your grandchild, how about preparing yourself? Registered childminders are required to undertake a paediatric first aid course. Why not do the same? These courses are widely available, take just one or two days, and are not unduly expensive. They cover things like dealing with falls, choking, drowning, burns and shocks. Look for one that provides practical hands-on training using models as well as taught theory and/or e-learning. Research has shown that in an emergency involving children, adults often do nothing, fearing to make matters worse, even though a few basic actions could save a life. It is all about knowing what to do. Knowledge drives out fear and the life you save could be your grandchild's.

Paediatric first aid courses are run by The Red Cross (**http://www.redcrossfirstaidtraining. co.uk**), St John's Ambulance (**www.sja.org.uk**) and several other organisations.

Catriona's friends were surprised when she went on a paediatric first aid course before taking on childcare responsibilities for her new granddaughter. As a doctor, they thought she would be well able to handle whatever was likely to happen. Catriona said, 'In my job I have never actually had to deal with a paediatric emergency. I was worried if anything happened, everyone would expect me to know what to do, but I wouldn't. I am much more confident now that I have had a chance to practise a few procedures under supervision.'

For a lot more about what to do when your grandchild is sick or has an accident, have a look at chapters 16 and 17.

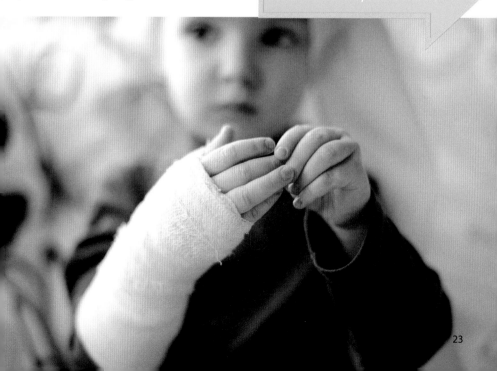

Routine and boundaries

P
L
A
N

Whatever the age of the child or children you are looking after, you will need a plan for the day. If you are looking after children of different ages, it is especially important to work out how the needs of each can be met in a way that gives you some sense of order and control.

A plan for the day

Nurseries have got structuring the day down to a fine art, with a basic routine adjusted for different age groups. The day revolves around set meal and nap times and the in-between times are filled with activities, some organised and some chosen by the individual child, some regular and some varying on a daily basis. They always make time for physical activity, imaginative play, outdoor play, singing and stories. Other activities include arts and crafts, music and dance, cooking, sand and water play. Play time and learning time are not distinguished from each other because young children learn through play.

A baby day

Handover

Before the parents disappear, make sure you have the baby's schedule written down, along with the latest on his likes and dislikes and any new developments.

Feeds and naps

Try your best to stick to your instructions, within reason. If your instructions are to wake the baby from a nap after a certain time, then do it, however peacefully the baby is sleeping. In between feeding the baby and putting him down for naps, plan some activities that give variety and interest to the day. Babies have a lot of learning to do and they get bored and frustrated if the opportunities aren't offered. For you too, some variety makes the time pass.

Outings

Plan at least one outing a day, come rain or shine. Babies love to be taken out, whether in a sling or a pushchair, and are easy to please as far as the destination goes. Decide what you would like to do, and take the baby along for the ride. If the baby is a good sleeper, schedule the outing for right after a nap, so she is awake to enjoy the change of scene. If not, then plan the outing for when you think she needs some help to doze off.

Song and dance time

Babies seem to love the human voice above all other sounds. They are spellbound when you sing to them, and they will enjoy listening to whatever kind of songs you enjoy singing. When they are old enough to hold a rattle you can get them to join in. Being carried, sung to, danced with and patted on the back all at the same time is baby heaven.

Watch and listen time

Babies love to watch what is going on. Before they can sit up by themselves, they enjoy a seat that props them up so they can see. There are now a wide range available, from bouncy chairs (be very careful and do not put one of these on a table – babies can quickly bounce themselves over the edge) to rubber tyres. When she is old enough to sit in a highchair, move the chair near where you are working, and let her watch and bang a spoon while you talk about what you are doing. If you are also looking after a toddler, put the baby where she can watch the older child playing but keep a close eye on them. Even the most loving of toddlers has been known to hit or bite a baby sibling.

Handing back

The parents will want to know how much the baby has had to eat and drink, what sort of mood he has been in and how long he napped. Be a little reticent to share your excitement about any milestones in his progress. It is more fun for the parents if they discover these advances for themselves. Imagine coming home from a tough day at work to hear that your baby has said his first word while you were in a meeting!

Toddlers and pre-schoolers

Handover

Ask the parents how the child has been since you last saw them and if there is anything special to look out for.

Meals

Routine is the key to establishing a sense of order and security, and meal times are the backbone of the routine. Nursery days usually start with breakfast or a snack which ensures that the children don't start the day hungry, especially if they refused to eat before they left home. The sight of food set out at little tables is inviting to the child and makes it easier for the parent to say goodbye. The same principles apply with childcare at home. Having a welcome meal or snack and drink all ready, in the child's special place with their own special crockery, will make them feel at home straight away. Meals should be social occasions, so sit and chat about any plans for the day while the child eats.

Plan to provide a meal or snack and drink every two hours, with nothing but water offered in between. That naturally divides the day into two-hour chunks, and you can plan your other activities accordingly.

Nap time

Children vary hugely in when and how much they sleep during the day. Late morning or after lunch are common times to need a rest. Make sure you have somewhere quiet and dark where the child can sleep, in a cot or on a mattress on the floor.

Nap times are a chance for you to get some chores done, or to put your feet up, unless of course you have another child to care for. An older sibling may greatly value some time to play quietly without the younger one ruining his games or may want your undivided attention for some special one to one time.

Physical activities

Children need plenty of physical activity to develop their muscles and bones and to learn motor control. Mornings are usually when they have the most energy, so this is the time to get them out in the garden if you have one, or down to the park, or anywhere they can run around and climb on things. On rainy days take them to a shopping centre or anywhere else you have locally where they can run about in the dry. Or dress them up in waterproofs and boots and get them out stamping in puddles.

Imaginative play time

If toddlers are with their peer group in a nursery, they will often enjoy parallel imaginative play, but they don't really play together the way pre-school children will. It is good for them to develop the ability to play with their toys alone, but don't expect it to last for long. It is often easier looking after two children than one, once they get to the stage of playing together. If they start squabbling, they are probably getting bored. Introduce a distracting activity rather than trying to police them.

Television

Before the age of three the evidence is that watching any television at all is detrimental to the child's development. Babies learn better from the real world than from a screen and screen time eats up the time available for real-world learning. DVDs designed to be educational for babies to teach them words are less effective than being read or talked to by a 'real person', and when the television is on, grown-ups spend less time interacting with the baby. With children over the age of three, a modest dose of television is not known to be harmful, although not as good for his development as getting physical exercise or playing, painting or reading. If you can manage not to resort to television at all, so much the better. If you feel you must have some down-time in the day to check your e-mails, make your phone calls or just relax now that the child has outgrown naps, scheduling in 30-60 minutes of age-appropriate television is unlikely to do harm. But be firm and consistent about when and what and don't extend the time in response to whines of 'I'm bored!' Don't have the television on in the background during the rest of the day. It is distracting for everyone.

Offering choices

Children love to feel they have some control over their lives. Within your schedule, offer the child choices, limited to the category of things that you had planned.

Five-year-old Lily was learning about luck and chance through playing snakes and ladders with her grandfather Richard. She also had a great sense of order and liked to discuss the plan for their day over breakfast. One day Richard suggested brainstorming a list of ideas for things to do. Out of the list they picked six things that both of them liked, some short and some quite time-consuming. Then Richard got Lily to throw the dice to decide the order in which they would do them. In the event, they managed to get them all done in the course of a frantic but highly enjoyable day.

Of course, if the children have become absorbed in an activity, don't disturb them for the sake of keeping to a schedule. Make sure the interest has not come from something you would rather they weren't doing (crayoning the table top, taking a pop-up book to pieces, exploring your phone) but otherwise leave them to it. Those moments are too precious to waste.

Try out different things and even if one activity is a roaring success, don't include it every time. You will probably end up being able to use that activity more often if you keep it a bit special and it might be a just what you need to brighten a rainy day. Chapters 5-12 are packed with ideas that have worked for us.

At the end of the day

Pack a 'home bag' with any toys and books your grandchild brought from home and any paintings, crafts or baked goods she made during the day. When you meet the parent, take a moment to say how the child has been, how well she behaved, and the things you did together. There is no need to tell tales about minor misbehaviours but do mention any events that have potential after effects. For example, if the child fell off the climbing frame and banged her head, the parents need to know so that they are on the lookout for delayed effects. If handing back is too rushed for this kind of conversation, try texting the highlights of the day and any amusing or interesting things the child has said. Parents love to know about their child's day and it gives them something to talk about with the child at bedtime.

Boundaries and discipline

In general, children behave well with their grandparents, especially in their grandparents' house. On their own territory they feel more secure and prepared to push the boundaries. You will probably find your grandchildren behave better with you than they do with their parents, or indeed than your children did with you. Generally speaking, if you give them the attention and praise they need, keep them busy, get them out and about with lots of exercise, and feed and water them regularly, they will behave pretty well.

Boundaries

Children do need some rules and boundaries and once they know what they are, they are likely to test them to make sure they are solid. It is important to be consistent and not to yield to moaning or whining. Your role is to be clear in your own mind what your rules are and to stick to them.

Family rules

Are there family rules about snacks or television that you should know about? If the rule is 'no sweets during the week', or 'no getting a new game out until the other one has been put away' then support the parents and stick to the same rules. Don't depend on the child telling you what the family rules are — it is too tempting for him to bend them in the telling.

Your rules

On the other hand there is no reason why you shouldn't have your own rules in your own house. Maybe Mummy does let the children bounce on her bed, or eat in front of the television, stay up late or leave their clothes all over the floor. In your house you are entitled to have your own rules. Once a child knows that 'But Mummy always lets me' provokes a wavering, that card will be played every time boundaries are imposed. Be prepared to give reasons but be firm and consistent. Don't expect the child to know how you want her to behave without being shown and seeing these behaviours modelled by you. As always, giving praise for getting things right is more effective than threats or punishments.

Dealing with challenging behaviour

You don't need us to tell you that smacking a child is no longer considered acceptable under any circumstances. Nor is yanking, pulling, pinching or verbally abusing. The shock of a smack may stop him doing something dangerous, but no more so than removing him promptly from the danger and explaining the reasons in a serious tone of voice. A democratic and reasoned approach works better than violence. Bad behaviour, however, should be seen to have consequences, so find out from the parents how they discipline their child and use the same approach if discipline proves necessary.

Distraction

There is no point in entering a battle of wills with a small child. Distraction is much more effective, and they soon grow out of the 'No!' stage. Don't ask questions that can be answered with 'No!' Don't let a conflict get out of hand, move on, 'Yes, you do need your nappy changed, so let's choose a toy to look at while we do it, do you want this bus or this car?' When you want the child to tidy his toys and he says 'No!' don't let him off the hook but don't make it into a scene either. If it's reasonable for it to be a job you can do together you can say, 'I will put these cars in the basket, can you get me that red one over there?'

Rewards

Don't use edible treats as a reward for good behaviour, as it sets up an inappropriate relationship with food. Most children are happy if their good behaviour is simply noticed and praised and they get hugs. It is good for a child to learn that the glow of virtue is a reward in itself.

Getting active

Children need lots of physical activity to develop their muscles and bones, balance and co-ordination. They also need it to develop their self-confidence, courage and resilience. Indoors or out, rain or shine, they need the freedom and encouragement to run about, climb and master physical challenges. Television and computers provide such addictive entertainment these days, that ensuring children get plenty of physical activity is more important than ever.

As a guide, young children should spend at least an hour a day being vigorously active: running, jumping, climbing, bouncing, dancing or playing ball. Obviously, they can't keep that kind of activity up for a straight 60 minutes, so plan to encourage several bursts of activity during the day. Some children never seem to keep still, but all the more reason to get them out of the house and running the fidgets out of their legs. Indications that it is time to get out and get active are whining, quarrelling with siblings or saying, 'I'm bored.'

Out and about

Walking

Try at least one walking expedition each day from the time your grandchild takes his first steps. Keep it well within his capability and don't take along anything for him to ride on. He may ask to be carried, but try distracting him. If all else fails, try running! A toddler who is too tired to walk is rarely too tired to run, especially if you make a game of it and run with him, holding his hand. By the age of two most children can happily manage a 20 minute walk and it is great exercise. The best kind of walk takes them somewhere interesting and a picnic snack will revive tired legs for the return journey..

Playgrounds and parks

Playgrounds offer an exciting range of physical experiences and challenge for children right from when they are able to sit up in a baby swing. There is a useful website that tells you where all the playgrounds are around where you live: **http://toolserver. org/~stephankn/playground**. Just locate your part of the country on the map and then click down to find the playgrounds in your area.

Explore your local area and talk to friends who have children for advice on where to go. There may be all kinds of play opportunities near you that you never really thought about, not having seen them through the eyes of a child.

> Natalie lived a short drive from a National Trust property. With her family membership, she could enter free with her two grandchildren as often as she liked. The children had no interest in seeing the house, but the rhododendron bushes in the garden proved a wonderful place for making dens and on a dry day they were always happy playing there for an hour or more.

Getting active indoors

Baby gym time

Even babies need exercise time. These days there are ingenious baby gyms made up of a colourful mat with an arch of little toys dangling just out of reach. The baby has something to look at and usually lies there happily kicking for 20 minutes or more. However, they are outgrown within a few months so may not be worth investing in unless you have the baby most days or there are other grandchildren on the way. A sheepskin rug, towel or cot blanket will do just as well and can be easily washed when the baby brings his milk up over it.

Take as much of his clothing off as is compatible with the temperature and basic hygiene: for some reason, the less he is wearing, the more he will kick and wave his arms around. Also, the more there is to look at or reach out for, the longer he will be happy to lie there. Place him somewhere with things to look at, close enough for him to see. A mobile made out of a hanger with silver foil strips taped to it works fine, hung in sight but out of reach. During baby gym time, stay close, check frequently that he is still happy, and don't leave him on the floor unsupervised for a millisecond if there are pets or other children about. Exercise time will last longer if you sit close and jiggle a series of intriguing objects just out of his reach. This can be a good time to make a phone call as the baby will enjoy hearing you talking, provided you smile and nod at him from time to time.

Tummy time

Babies need to lie on their tummies for a few minutes each day to help them develop head control and strengthen their arms ready for crawling. Now that babies are always put on their backs to sleep, it is important to schedule this in. Some babies love tummy time and happily arch up their heads to look around. However, quite a few just hate it and howl and some just put their heads down and fall asleep immediately. Don't leave the baby sleeping on his tummy. Roll him over onto his back - it is the safest position for babies to sleep.

Creeping and rolling

A baby who is beginning to shift around inside her cot needs space to practise rolling over and thrashing about on a blanket on the floor during the day. Try providing incentives in the form of a circle of toys, all just out of reach, for her try to inch towards. She may be planning to head for one toy but find she has somehow gone into reverse gear, so it is a nice surprise when she finds she has moved closer to another!

Babies can't start to crawl or walk until their nervous system is developed enough to give them the necessary motor control for these complex movements. That happens at differing rates: some start crawling at four months, some not until nine months, some never crawl and go straight to walking. They all feel the instinct to move, but they just can't do it until their bodies are ready, and late movers can get quite frustrated. Baby bouncers don't speed the motor development along, but they do provide ten or 15 minutes at a time of entertainment and physical activity for a baby at this awkward age. Babies at this stage also adore being held while they practise standing or being 'walked' with both their hands held. Your back will probably limit how long you can keep that up for.

Baby on the move

When a baby starts to crawl he can get carpet burn on his knees. It looks like a rash but dies down quite quickly and the skin soon toughens up. Trousers that cover the knees help, but you may want to engage him in some other activity for the rest of the day and give the knees a chance to settle down.

As soon as he can pull himself up, arrange the furniture into a cruising circuit so he can travel about the whole room holding on. Place favourite toys at strategic intervals and watch him manoeuvre round the room from one to the next.

Encourage him to develop his stair-climbing skills while you sit on the step just below, in case of slippage. Your stairs are bound to be intriguingly different from the ones at home. (Don't forget to put the safety gates up before you think they will be needed, and keep them locked securely until he is safe going up and down by himself.)

Toddler runs

Toddlers love to practise their toddling skills so just push the furniture aside to create a clear track which is big enough to encourage him to move. If you can create a circular run, going through more than one room, so much the better. Chasing and being chased round in circles is endless and exhausting fun, and something grandfathers may be especially good at. Dragging a wooden pull toy makes it even more fun, if you don't mind your furniture being bashed about. A teddy on a string is less damaging.

Action rhymes

Action rhymes and games are great for encouraging different movements. 'Ring a ring a roses' is a sure-fire hit, but be prepared for it to wear you out more quickly than it used to when you were the parent. 'Sleeping bunnies' is a much better choice if you are feeling fragile, as all you have to do is sing it while the child does all the work. If you don't know this one, try doing an internet search for 'Sleeping bunnies' and look at some of the renditions on YouTube. This is a great way to remind yourself of the words and tunes of favourite children's songs. Whatever ones you think of are almost certain to be on YouTube.

Angela entertains her two-year old granddaughter by singing up to five rounds of 'Sleeping bunnies' while giving the baby his morning feed. By the time the baby is put down, the exhausted toddler is ready for a nap herself.

Fun on the furniture

Make up your mind about your attitude to climbing on furniture. If it's a 'no', and you mean it, then make that clear from the start and be consistent. This is likely to be a rule that is frequently challenged and if you relent once, you have lost the battle for good. Your favourite sofa will become your grandchild's favourite climbing frame. The same goes for using your bed as a trampoline. Of course if you really don't mind (that old sofa was due for dumping anyway) there is a lot of fun and great exercise to be had from clambering about on your furniture.

Disco dancing

Children of every age love to dance to music and learn new dance moves, so clear a space, put on your own favourite dance-floor fillers and have some fun together until you collapse out of breath. You could even plan a show for Mummy!

Indoor Olympics

Children love a challenge, as long as there is lots of praise and no criticism for failed attempts. Try laying a long piece of ribbon or string on the carpet, or draw a chalk mark on a suitable hard floor, and see if she can walk along it without stepping off. When she can, see if she can do it with a small bean bag or a floppy toy on her head. You try too, maybe with a book on your head: give yourself a challenge!

Slalom races are fun, with the course weaving among cushions on the floor, or corridor races if you have a long corridor. Time how long it takes the child to complete the course, counting loudly, and see if they can beat their own personal best. The nice thing is they usually can, since they keep on developing and growing.

Other good indoor activities are: pretending to be hopping frogs or bunnies, learning how to do somersaults, playing musical bumps, and seeing how long they can keep a balloon in the air. Joining in and giving lots of praise for every achievement is needed to keep these games going long enough to wear the child out.

In the garden

If you are lucky enough to have any kind of garden, it will probably be the focus of the child's interest. The space and freedom of being outdoors encourages running around without need for much in the way of equipment or toys, especially if there is another child or a dog to play with. If you have a child on her own she will need more encouragement to get active. See also the section on Garden safety in Chapter 3.

Play equipment

The garden provides a great space for hide and seek, hopscotch, treasure hunts, races and ball games, all of which need minimal equipment. Having a few props to add variety will keep children outside and interested for even longer.

Provide a plastic watering can and some child-size but functioning gardening tools and encourage your grandchild to work by your side. This can be a lot of fun, giving her little pointers about how to hold the tools properly and snippets of information about the fruit, vegetables and flowers as you work on them. Show her how to use her small tools and praise her efforts. A bonus is that children are rarely fussy about eating food that they have planted, watered, cleaned and cooked for a meal. In fact, they are very proud of their achievement, and the food tastes so much the better!

The garden is great for learning how to do big challenging activities like sweeping, raking, hosing, digging, mowing, shovelling snow and gathering fruit, vegetables or flowers. Involve her in your work in the garden when she is little and she may even grow to be a genuine help.

John rigged a clothes line, securely tied between two trees, at a height that was over his toddler grandson Joey's head, so he wouldn't run into it, but that he could just reach. Joey had a great time with it, stretching up to attach clothes pegs, taking them down again, running for more pegs. When John's older grandchildren came to stay, it became first a washing line for doll's clothes and then the central support for a tent made out of an old double sheet.

Big play equipment will undoubtedly make the garden more interesting to play in, but think before you buy. Things to consider before ordering are safety, cost, size, play value and durability. Safety is relative: bumps, bruises and minor injuries are all part of growing up, but you won't want to buy a climbing frame that looks as if it might collapse under a bit of rough and tumble. In general you get what you pay for, but in the world of climbing frames and swing sets, make sure the value is in the sturdiness rather than the number of play features.

Really good swings and climbing frames are lots of fun, and will occupy two or more children for hours. But they cost a lot, they take up a lot of room in the garden, they are less fun for a child on her own, and it is hard to find equipment suitable for toddlers that pre-school children will still enjoy. Having those things at home may make a walk to use similar equipment in the local playground less appealing. If you have a convenient tree, hanging a swing or a knotted rope securely from a suitable strong branch provides lots of fun while being cheaper and less obtrusive.

Trampolines

Trampolines are very popular with children but good ones are expensive and you will want the safest kind with full safety netting and covered springs. RoSPA have useful guidance on their website **www.rospa.com/leisuresafety/adviceandinformation/leisuresafety/trampoline-safety.aspx** about safety in setting up a trampoline and making sure it doesn't sail off in a strong wind. Children under six shouldn't be allowed on a trampoline that is designed for older children or adults. They must not be allowed to go on with another person (or the dog) as that is how most injuries occur and they must not be allowed to attempt somersaults or flips, or to bounce off at the end when they have finished. You have to supervise children at all times when they are bouncing. Trampolining is great fun and great exercise and children do need to learn to take risks, but unless you are into trampolining yourself, you may feel that this is an activity you could leave them to discover with their parents.

You could consider buying a garden-size bouncy castle, just right for one or two under-fives to jump around in. They are reasonably priced, inflate in minutes, and have the advantage of packing away surprisingly small. The child has to be supervised at all times, of course, and will tire of the activity after ten to 15 minutes jumping. But what with the whole drama of getting it out and inflated, and then down and packed away, a bouncy castle can provide a useful highlight for an afternoon in the garden.

Cheaper options that will still make your garden a magnet and get the children running around like mad things are little football goal nets, beach game sets, toy wagons, ride-ons and wheelbarrows. These can all be picked up cheaply in charity shops, at car boot sales or off the internet, but you won't be able to store too many of them. Don't get anything your grandchildren already have in their own home.

The best plaything of all is an enthusiastic grandparent. The more you join in, the longer the fun will last and the more energy everyone will burn off. And you will all have a great appetite for your tea!

Annie had a small garden that she did not want cluttered up when the grandchildren weren't there. She invested in outdoor toys that were fun for them when they visited but which she could dismantle or deflate and store in her garden shed when they went home. These included:

★ inflatable animals (a dragon and a crocodile) really meant for riding on in swimming pools but brilliant on the grass for bouncing and imaginative play

★ a small easy-to-erect tent

★ inflatable child-size sofa beds

★ child-size folding camping stools and table

★ inflatable beach balls.

Words and stories

By the time children turn five they have learned an amazing amount about how the world works. They can speak at least one language fluently, can make sense of abstract symbols like letters and numbers and have a grasp of practical physics. Their minds are as absorbent as blotting paper, and there are so many things they seem to be able to pick up with ease at this age that sometimes become a struggle later.

Absorbent minds

For babies and small children, discovering about the world and the way it works is fascinating and they take it in without effort. They are absorbing everything around them and accepting that what they experience is the way things are and should be. Exposure to beauty in nature and art, music and dance help them to see these as normal and natural. They will also be absorbing the way people communicate with each other and show affection, the rhythms of the languages they speak, and the culture into which they have been born. By the age of six months a baby can already tell when a grown-up is just being silly and it will make her laugh.

Sensitive periods

There are times when a child is particularly sensitive to learning certain things, and will pursue these with great concentration and passion. In evolutionary terms, this passion for learning makes total sense. The sooner a child is able to understand her environment enough to make sure her needs are met and she can recognise danger and call for help or move away, the better her survival chances.

Sensitive periods for learning

Birth to four years	Movement
Birth to five years	Refinement of the senses
Birth to six years	Language
One to two years	Order
Two to six years	Number
Four to six years	Manners and courtesy

Senses

A baby has a strong urge to work out what is going on around him. His five senses are there to tell him about his environment, but he has had little opportunity to develop them in the womb. Now he has to learn quite complex things like which faces belong to people who take care of him and which don't. Have you ever noticed the intensity with which a baby looks at you when he is being fed? Picking up a crying baby to comfort him is another way of telling him that his messages have been received and he can count on you to work out the problem. This is very reassuring to the baby and a great bonding opportunity for a grandparent.

Babies start to make associations. They learn things like the sound of running water means bathtime, a darkened room means time to sleep, the smell of mashed banana means time to eat. Over the first few years all the senses develop, and the child will enjoy learning about the smell, taste, and feel of all kinds of things as well as the sights and sounds and, having learned, will want to move on.

Michelle looked after baby Larry one afternoon a week in her flat. As soon as he arrived, she carried him from room to room, explaining what happened in each place. One day she noticed he wriggled and twisted round when they passed certain pictures on the wall, so after that she would stop and talk to him about the pictures and he seemed fascinated. After about two months of this, he stopped paying attention to the pictures, and just squirmed to get down, so she stopped the ritual.

Following the child

What isn't fun for children (or anyone else) is being instructed about things they don't want to know, being told they are wrong, or being expected to stick at something after they have lost interest. It is possible to give children a distaste for anything 'educational' if you can't stop yourself doing those things. On the other hand if you let the child take the lead, encourage his interests, praise his achievements and let him decide when he is ready to move on, he will master one skill after another and grow in self-esteem and confidence on the way.

Society and culture

Children need to know how the world works so when you are out and about point out what jobs people are doing. The window cleaner abseiling down the side of a building, the postman emptying the pillar box. Talk to the child about what sort of job she would like to do when she grows up, what jobs you have done, what her parents do. Talk to her about your memories of 'olden times' when you were young, and how things are done differently in other countries.

Barbara had a ten minute walk to the station to pick up her two-year-old grandson Seth. After the first few times, she decided not to try to hurry him along, but to let him set the pace. They stopped to look at shop windows and talked about what presents they might buy for all his family next Christmas. They looked at delivery vans unloading and speculated about what the restaurants would be serving for lunch. By the time they got to her flat, Seth had already had a stimulating time and was ready for some quiet play.

Literacy and language

Children who are cared for by grandparents tend to have a wider vocabulary than other children. Each generation uses language a bit differently, and grandparents may use words not so often used at home or at nursery. Build on this advantage by talking to your grandchild as well as listening to him. Tell him about what his father or mother used to get up to when they were his age, a sure-fire hit. Don't worry about using long words, after all most children can reel off dinosaur names, but make sure the meaning of the new word is clear from the context, and include it in a few sentences during the day to help make the learning stick.

The key to encouraging literacy and language is to read and talk with the child. Babies have a strong urge to listen to people talking. It used to be said that you should talk to babies in a normal conversational voice, but the universal instinct to talk to young babies in special high-pitched 'baby-talk' is now reckoned to be just what they need. Your grandchild will love the sound of your voice, especially when he can see that you are talking or singing to him. He will love being cuddled on your lap and read to, right from the early weeks.

You may find it harder to understand your toddler grandchild than you expect. Part of the trouble is that your hearing deteriorates with age and his articulation is only just developing. You may not catch everything he says even if he does say it properly. Be patient with him and he will be patient with you: the main thing to get across is your willingness to listen and to understand.

Toddlers make lots of mistakes as they learn to talk, and don't enjoy being told they have got it wrong. The best way of encouraging improvement is to respect the attempt, try to work out what was meant and then repeat it correctly, so if the child says 'Granny milk!' nod understandingly and repeat back to him, 'Milk please, Granny?'.

Some people worry that it will confuse a child if he is exposed to more than one language. In fact children up to the age of six or seven are very good at picking up different languages and using them with the appropriate people, as long as they hear them spoken regularly. At this age, languages are easy to learn, whereas later it is harder to shape new sounds.

Learning about words

By the age of three most children have grasped that pictures and words are different ways of expressing meaning. They get the concept of stories and are happy to tell the story themselves from the pictures and memory of the sounds, without looking at the words. Later they start to recognize that the words contain important information. At this stage, when adults go through a picture book talking about the pictures rather than reading the text, they may say sternly, 'read the WORDS!'.

Nathan and his grandmother had made gingerbread men together. Having laid them out on the table to cool, Nana said, 'Let's go to the park.'

Nathan: 'Yes. It will be all right to just leave them there.'

Nana (teasing): 'You don't think they will run away then?'

Nathan (looking all around the room with exaggerated care): 'I don't see any words! This isn't a story!'

The idea that words can do more than tell a story makes learning to read appealing to the child who is more interested in facts than fiction. A great way of encouraging the concept that words serve a useful purpose is to raise children's awareness of signs when you are out and about.

Jago knew his letters but was more interested in trains than in books. Kathryn got him interested in deciphering signs when they were out. He was soon able to let her know whether smoking was banned here, or bicycles permitted there, and what the fine would be if your dog did a poo in the park. When they travelled by underground Jago found that Kathryn was completely hopeless at finding the way to the right line without his help, and if he hadn't spotted the 'Way Out' signs they would probably still be down there. Once he saw the point of it, his reading came on a treat.

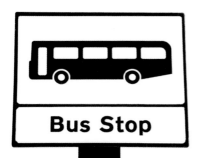

Bus Stop

Books, books, books

The most important way you can help your grandchild to read is to develop his love of books. Make storytime a regular daily event and be prepared to let him choose what you read, even if you have read it a hundred times before. Even a baby will indicate which books he likes, by batting away the rejects. Have plenty for him to choose from, and freshen your selection by picking up books at charity shops, local fêtes or by trips to the library. Get a mix of fiction and non-fiction, following his interests. Make storytime his special time when you pay him full attention and give him lots of praise for pointing things out or guessing what will happen next.

Learning to read

From around age three, your grandchild is likely to start wanting to learn to read for himself and may appreciate your help. You are not his teacher, but you will want to help him learn this vital skill if he is showing interest. Current thinking is that the best way is to start with phonics: the sounds that letters or combinations of letters make. Start with lowercase letters and leave the capitals for later, except for the letter that starts his name. The first step is for him to recognise each letter and the sound it usually makes. It helps the child to learn the shape of each letter as it would be used in joined-up writing, right from the start. Sandpaper lower case cursive letters that he can trace with his finger and feel as well as see are used in Montessori schools and you can get these online from a range of suppliers though they are quite expensive. There are also plenty of phonics workbooks with bright pictures and enjoyable exercises available.

Once he has mastered the letters and the sounds they make, you can teach him the common two-letter combinations, like oo, oi, ai, sh, ch and th. He will need these to start reading because common words are full of

them. After that it is a matter of making it fun to work out what you get when you put one sound next to another sound and blend them. This is like a puzzle and it can be fun with lots of praise and encouragement and no criticism or impatience. If it isn't fun, just drop it and go back to reading books together. Let the child set the pace.

Writing

As your grandchild's hand-eye co-ordination and dexterity develop she will enjoy challenges like dot-to-dot puzzles and drawing a line between matching pictures. Following the lines of a maze or tangle are other fun 'puzzles' that help her get ready to write. Try writing her name in dots, and encourage her to join them up, starting at the top left hand corner, to write her name.

Once she is beginning to get the idea, encourage her by helping her write shopping lists, to-do lists, labels for her toys, messages for her parents and menus for her tea parties. Even if she only dictates them for you to write, she is still learning about capturing and communicating ideas by writing them down.

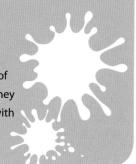

Arts, crafts and music

A day of childcare is rarely complete without at least one session of arts and crafts. Even babies enjoy making their mark, as soon as they are old enough to grip a crayon. Don't leave under-threes alone with drawing material though, as bits of bitten off crayon, the tops of pens and chunks of glue stick can all be choking hazards.

Arts

Drawing

Once your grandchild has passed the stage of chewing everything, keep a basket of materials in an accessible place so that he can get it out without help when the urge to be creative strikes him. The basket should contain paper and a manageable number of non-toxic washable felt-tip pens. Most children prefer felt-tip pens to coloured pencils and crayons because they make a stronger impact. Check from time to time that the pens all work, and add some new ones when they're needed. The basket shouldn't be so full that it has to be tipped out before the child can find what he needs, or filled up with bits of broken crayons and other rubbish.

Have a special low table and chair for him to sit at, or cover the kitchen or dining room table with a smooth plastic tablecloth. He should know there is a place where he is allowed to settle down for a spot of drawing at any time the urge takes him. Encourage him to put the tops on his pens when he has finished using them. Some children like to have a drawing on the go all day, coming back to it periodically, so don't be in a hurry to tidy it away unless space is at a premium.

Painting

Painting is a different kind of creativity from drawing. You need more room for more sweeping strokes, and a bigger sheet of paper to work on. Poster paints in sets of little pots are very appealing and a new set will be greeted with joy, but the tiny amounts provided make them poor value for money. At best you get three sessions out of one set, and that is only if you spoon a third of each pot onto a plate or palette. If you just give the pots and a brush to an exuberant three-year old, you will have plenty of paint left at the end of one session, but it will all be brown. The cheapest way of buying paints is in powder form, but it can be fiddly and time-consuming to mix it up. The best option if you have a keen painter is to buy big pots of poster paints from one of the online arts and crafts companies such as Baker Ross, who have a good range with appealing colours.

Raj loved to paint. His grandmother bought some big bottles of non-toxic poster paints, a pad of A3 painting paper and assorted brushes from an online supplier. Every time he came, she offered him his choice of colours and he helped to squeeze them onto the old muffin tray that served for a palette. He loved to mix his colours in the empty sections of the tray and decide what his inventions were called. Each picture he painted went through a phase of being very beautiful with colourful swirls and dots, and then, as he worked on, less and less so. His mother, presented at the end of the day with yet another sheet of thick purplish-brown paint had difficulty understanding why Raj and his grandmother were so enthusiastic, but as his grandmother said, 'It is the process that matters, not the product.'

Magic pictures

A fun thing to do for a change is to give the child a wax candle to draw an invisible picture and then paint over with watery poster paint to reveal the picture. If you have a sheet of coloured Cellophane, ask the child to draw a picture in the same colour on some white paper, place the Cellophane on top and the picture will disappear! Or get the child to scribble all over a sheet of paper with crayons of every colour. Add some more yourself to make sure the wax is thickly laid on. Get her to paint the paper with an even layer of black poster paint and let it dry. Now take a fork and scrape off some of the paint to reveal amazing firework-like patterns.

Paper

There is nothing like a sheet of crisp clean white paper to stimulate a child's desire to paint or draw but it can be expensive to provide, especially when children are at the age when they make one scribble and then want a new piece. You can buy rolls of paper but they can be a false economy because the edges curl up annoyingly. If you have a source of scrap paper that has been printed on one side only, use that. If not, the best value is probably one of those big packs of A4 paper for computer printers.

Modelling

As soon as the child is old enough not to eat it, try introducing modelling material. Making your own play dough has the advantage that you make what you need on the day and don't have to store it. The basic recipe is equal measures of flour and hot water with half a measure of salt. That sounds like a lot of salt, but the salt is what holds the water in the mixture and keeps it from being sticky. A bit of vegetable oil and cream of tartar add elasticity and smoothness and cooking improves the texture. There are lots of ways to vary the basic recipe, like adding glitter for sparkles or sand or oatmeal for texture. Don't add anything that makes it smell like food (vanilla essence, cocoa powder etc) as play dough is not safe to eat. You can store the dough in an airtight container and reuse it, but more likely the child will want to take her creations home to show Mummy and making a fresh batch next time with new colours will be more fun.

A recipe for perfect play dough

- 1 cup plain flour
- ½ cup table salt
- 1 tablespoon vegetable oil
- ½ tablespoon of cream of tartar

Put it all in a saucepan. Add a cup of hot water, stir and put on a low heat to cook. Stir while cooking until the mixture forms itself into a ball in the middle of the pan (3-5 minutes). Tip the ball out onto a smooth clean surface, knead and divide into 4-6 smaller balls, depending on how many colours you want. Add colour by moulding the dough into a bowl shape, dropping a little food colouring into the centre, folding the dough over and kneading well. Pastel colours are pretty and take less colouring.

Plasticine is a perennial favourite. It is a bit hard for little hands to knead it to malleability, so you will have to do this, but it rolls out well when softened, and is good for cutting shapes out of, for example with pastry cutters. Plasticine needs changing from time to time, once the colours have got marbled together and bits of grit have become embedded. Special sets of tools, moulds or presses to go with the play dough or Plasticine are sure-fire winners.

A relatively new product is a light-weight supersoft modelling clay that dries hard over a couple of days. It comes in vibrant colours or in pure white that can be painted once it has dried. It is wonderfully easy to use and a winner with children of four years or older. Available from internet arts and crafts suppliers it is comparatively expensive so it is only worth it if your grandchild is a keen modeller and interested in producing something that will last.

Making things is a great way of developing concentration, hand-eye co-ordination and a sense of self-esteem. Don't attempt anything too complicated, you will just end up making it yourself while the children make a camp under the table!

For decorating purposes (provided there are no under-threes around) bring out a box of little buttons, ribbons, shells, sequins, bits of wool etc which you have collected for that purpose. Don't try to stick these on with glue sticks as they will just fall off again. You need something stronger like PVA glue, or else re-stick the decorations later when your grandchild is doing something else.

Crafts

Origami can be great fun, and children love to learn how to make paper boats or aeroplanes. If you aren't an adept at this, there are plenty of books on origami for children so this could be a new skill for both of you.

The thing children enjoy more than anything is making a present for their mummy or daddy. Craft shops and internet suppliers have a huge range of small plain boxes, plates, mugs, photo frames etc that can be decorated as gifts. Variety is important as even a small child knows Mummy won't want more than half a dozen boxes to keep her paper clips in, however beautifully embellished.

Other craft options include fabric paints to make bags or T-shirts, masks for painting and decorating, and themed items to make for special times of year. Good choices are little wooden models that can be painted up and then played with, white flowerpots that can be decorated and filled with a small plant to make a present and doll's house furniture. Flat wooden figures on sticks or wooden pegs are fun to decorate and can then be used for a puppet show: all you need for a theatre is a cardboard box with a slit in the bottom for them to pop through.

Safety note

Even when your grandchild is past the age of chewing everything, she may be tempted to put pens or brushes in her mouth or suck an ink-stained thumb. Don't buy arts and crafts materials that are not marked as suitable for children and observe any age restrictions. Pens, inks, paints and glues may contain substances that can be absorbed through the skin as well as the mouth, and children are much more susceptible to their effects than adults.

Don't use anything not sold as a skin paint to paint the skin. Don't combine arts and crafts time with snack time, and wash up your grandchild, yourself and all the surfaces used before serving food or drink. More on arts and crafts safety can be found on this website: **http://www.poison.vcu.edu/pdfs/ art_products.pdf**

Music

If you love music yourself, share this with your grandchildren just the way you did with your own children. Bells, a tambourine or some maracas make great accompaniments to a singing session with babies and toddlers, and they will enjoy having an instrument to shake or bang. A sing-along with the guitar, showing them the notes on a recorder or sitting them on your lap to try out the piano will all be exciting and fun activities. Don't turn them into music lessons unless specifically asked to by the parents as you want to remain the grandparent and not become the music teacher. Keep it at the level of exploration, entertainment, and enjoyment, with all efforts recognised and praised.

Songs

It seems to be a universal instinct to sing to children and no doubt you will remember the songs that were sung to you and those you sang to your own children. It doesn't much matter what you sing or how badly, but it is useful to have a repertory of songs that are not the same as the ones Mummy sings, both for variety and to avoid comparisons (which will not usually be in your favour). You will definitely want a book of nursery rhymes, and if you have forgotten the tunes, get a CD or DVD compilation or try YouTube.

Fay had songs for every occasion with her own children and these came back to her with the grandchildren. There were getting dressed songs, breakfast songs, waiting songs, going home songs, running songs, bath songs and bedtime songs. The going home songs were particularly useful to keep tired little legs moving, and included 'Show me the way to go home', 'Swing low, sweet chariot' and 'This old man came rolling home.'

Numbers and science

Research has shown that children cared for by grandparents are not as ready for school as those who have formal nursery education, and it is particularly in maths and science that we do less well. Maybe these topics feel more like teaching than childcare, or grandparents are not sure how to approach them.

Maths all around

Counting songs are a good start to learning about numbers: 'One, two, buckle my shoe' can start the first time you carry your baby grandchild upstairs, and every time thereafter. Songs that count forward, like 'This old man...' or 'One, two three, four, five...' are better to start with than the ones that count backward, like 'Ten little monkeys.' There are lots of counting books and counting games available. With an older child board games like snakes and ladders are great for teaching counting as you can encourage him to touch each square as he moves his piece along. Count for him at first, and as soon as he gets the idea, get him counting for you.

Shapes are also an important mathematical concept. Cut out a set of two-dimensional shapes from stiff card and talk about their names. Then go on to find these shapes around the house, outside and in picture books. Find or construct three-dimensional shapes like cones and cylinders to make a rocket, and use spheres for planets and then talk about them.

Learning about numbers, shapes and volume goes well with daily routines like mealtimes. Laying the table is a great way of getting a child to understand the important concept of sets as well as numbers: three forks, three knives, three spoons. When preparing food get him to calculate how many pieces of broccoli or fish fingers you need to cook. Give him a bowl of dried pasta or rice, a measuring cup and a spoon and show him how high you want the cup filled. Let him measure the cold water, pour it into the pan and then add the pasta/rice.

Our food

Food is interesting at every age. The fruit bowl is full of fascination for a baby who is sitting in a highchair, and he may reach out for it. If so, let him play with one or two pieces of fruit. He will find that an orange is like a ball, but it has an intriguing smell and texture and weight and it rolls around the tray in an interesting way; an apple is fragrant too, but has a different smell, and it doesn't roll anything like so well, and it is cool and smooth to touch; a banana is just the right shape for gripping and waving about. Sit with the child and enjoy a cup of tea while he explores the fruit. Talk to him about it – he understands more than you think!

An older child will be interested in where the fruit or vegetable has come from, why it is good for you, whether it grew in the ground or on a tree, what it looks like when you cut it one way or another. Let him wash baby carrots with a brush and get to know the texture. What is the string at one end for and why is there a stalk at the other end? Save one uncooked carrot for him to compare with a cooked one. What is different? What happened to it?

Babies and very young children enjoy the sensation of patting, poking and squeezing semi-solid food, as is clear from the moment they manage to get their hands into their food. This is learning for them, however messy. As they spread it around they are discovering all kinds of useful things about the properties of semi-solids and how they are different from solids and liquids. Try putting a few spoonfuls of chocolate pudding or jelly on the highchair tray and let him try to pick it up, poke it, splat it and generally smear it about. This is best done after he has been fed, so he won't be desperately trying to eat it, but it won't matter if some gets into his mouth.

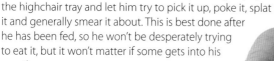

Water play

Water play is hugely appealing to babies and toddlers and a great way of entertaining them on a hot day, when it won't matter if they get soaked. They will enjoy discovering what sort of things float and what things sink, what happens to water in a container with holes in it and what happens to a stream of water if you put your hand in the way. Of course they can enjoy water play at bathtime too.

With an older child, try showing her how surface tension works. You can point out how insects seem to ride on the surface of the water. Sprinkle pepper on the surface of water in a glass and see how it floats, then add a drop of detergent and see what happens. Add a drop of food colour to another glass of water and then a drop of olive oil. Why does one mix in and the other not? Show her signs of condensation, on the windows of a steamy kitchen or if she breathes on a mirror or shiny metal. What happens to the outside of a glass

if you fill it with ice cubes? Help her discover about boiling, steam, evaporation and freezing by showing her examples of these around the house and out of doors. The properties of liquids are fascinating and mysterious even to adults. Share the wonder!

The human body

Talking about the five senses is a good start. Play a game where you give your grandchild some things in a cloth bag, to identify without looking at them, to show how much we learn from touch. Get her to identify tastes and then see what happens when she pinches her nose. Talk about how things smell and sound: play 'Guess who?' Do 'Spot the difference' puzzles and jigsaws and talk about looking at things carefully.

The next time your grandchild has a minor cut that bleeds, and you have washed it and comforted her, talk about it. Tell her about blood, what it is for, how it goes round the body, why a cut bleeds and why it stops bleeding. Let her feel your pulse and show her how to feel her own.

Talk about her bones, what they are for, how they hold us up, what they are made of. Show her how she can feel some of her own bones, and what they are called. Talk about what foods make bones strong, and how much bigger your bones are than hers.

Magnets

Lots of fun can be had with magnets. Most pre-schoolers will be familiar with fridge magnets and the magnets that hold engines and their carriages together in popular train sets. Try getting hold of an old-fashioned horseshoe magnet and demonstrate all the old familiar tricks with paper clips. It's fun and it's physics!

Space

The sun and moon and stars are there to be seen and wondered about and the planets and space travel, rockets and satellites are all exciting ideas for children to consider. How high could I jump on the moon? How long would it take to walk to space? To the moon? To the sun?

Marcia was telling her daughter about the morning she spent with the grandchildren at the Science Museum, and the questions that four-year-old Sophie had asked. She had started with, 'Grandma, what is Mars for?' Marcia had done her best, but one thing had led to another and she had ended up explaining the Big Bang theory. Her daughter said, 'Just now all conversations with Sophie end up with explaining the Big Bang theory!'

Why, why, why?

Children love asking questions and will go on and on as long as you have the patience to answer. If you don't know the answer, show the child how you can find these things out. A good children's encyclopaedia is a help here, and the internet is another great resource.

Bob's wife had taken the grandchildren to the Butterfly House, and they came home full of their experiences and clutching gift-shop toys. Sam's was a chameleon with a coiled tongue that shot out if you squeezed it. He climbed on Bob's knee to demonstrate his treasure, displacing Bob's laptop, and started to ask all kinds of questions about chameleons that Bob couldn't answer. Suppressing the urge to shoo him away while he finished his emails, Bob entered 'chameleon facts for children' on his browser. Together they discovered a wealth of information that fascinated both of them and chameleons became a running topic for the rest of the day.

Helping round the house

Small children love to learn how to do grown-up things all by themselves. You can help by taking the time to show them the proper way to do these things and letting them practise and learn without pressure. By involving them in some of your daily tasks you provide them with activity, interest and self-confidence. You may even make some small progress with the chores themselves.

Outdoor clothes

Provide a low peg so that your grandchild can hang up his own coat when he arrives. Show him how to hang it up by the loop at the top, and place his outside shoes neatly, toes pointed to the wall. Make sure you and your partner obey the same rules.

When it is time to go out again, teach him how to put his coat on. There is an easy way which most children enjoy learning. The child lays the coat on the floor with the hood end at his feet, the arms laid out sideways, and the front open. He bends down and slides his arms into both sleeves, then lifts the coat with his arms still stretched out and flings it over his head. Even the hood should fall into place, as by magic.

Dressing up

Indoor clothes are usually easier to put on and take off, and if you can acquire a few costumes for dressing up, the child will get plenty of opportunity to practise doing this. Our grandchildren seemed to prefer readymade superhero or princess costumes, rather than doing something imaginative with old scarves and hats. These costumes can be bought cheaply off the internet or in toyshops and are designed to be easy to put on and take off. Whether you can get them back into their day clothes, or are prepared to take a little Spiderman or Cinderella to the supermarket, is another matter!

Cleaning and tidying

Sweeping the floor

This is a good activity for developing control of large muscle groups (gross motor skills), and is especially fun if you provide small versions of adult equipment. Beware of wooden sets where the chunky dustpan doesn't actually work, or sets involving a trolley unless your kitchen has plenty of space to store it.

The secret of teaching a child how to do a task like this is to break it down into 'points of interest.' These steps will seem obvious to you, but are not clear to the child until explained and demonstrated in this kind of detail.

1. Look at the floor and see that there are bits of dust or rubbish to be cleaned up.

2. Take the broom and sweep the dust into one heap.

3. Put the broom away so it won't fall down.

4. Hold the dustpan on the floor with one hand and grip its small brush with the other.

5. Sweep the dust into the pan leaving none behind.

6. Carry the pan to the bin without dropping anything (a child's grasp of gravity is not so great).

Talk about each point of interest, 'Look, you got all the dust in a little pile', 'Now the dust is all in the pan!', 'See, you haven't dropped even one tiny bit!' This way the child is proud that he has achieved each step and is reminded of the overall aim of the activity. If your grandchild has special needs, try just giving him one of the steps to do, performing the others yourself and talking about what you are doing. Slowly build on success by getting him to do more steps and praise his progress.

Polishing

Most children love polishing. Ask your grandchild to sit at a table and polish a pair of your (old) shoes. Put newspaper underneath, roll his sleeves up and put on his painting gear as this can get messy. Ask him which colour matches the shoes best. Give him a demo on the use of polish and buffing to get a shine. Show him the 'points of interest' in first applying the polish to all the upper parts of the shoe, and then removing all trace of the cream or polish with the brush and buffing cloth. Praise each element that he manages, point out how nice the shoes now look, and help him clear up.

Washing up

Your grandchild will love to stand at a low table or on a stool at the sink, 'doing the washing up'. The warm, soapy water feels good, and it is fun to swirl a cloth around in it and pour water from one dish to another. Remind him that the aim is having a clean dish at the end of all this. Let him handle a few pieces of sturdy glass and crockery. There is a risk of the odd dish or cup being dropped and maybe broken so don't entrust him with your best things, but the concept that some things break if dropped is worth learning.

Pouring

Try asking your grandchild to fill an empty ice-cube tray from a jug of water, or pour juice into a glass. The 'points of interest' are seeing if the receiving container is filled just right, if any liquid was spilt and whether the pouring jug was partly or fully emptied in the process. He will learn how much control is needed to fill each utensil and get a feel for volume and the properties of liquids at the same time.

Other kitchen jobs

See what other tools you have that he could use: mop, bucket, duster, cleaning cloths, a plastic bowl for washing the cloths. He will find it quite absorbing to be using tools to do jobs.

Maria enjoyed baking and encouraged her grandson Ricardo to help her. She found a lovely set of child-size but functional baking utensils, complete with a small whisk, spatula, spoons, measuring cup, rolling pin and cutters. The next time they made biscuits together, Ricardo used each of his new tools with obvious satisfaction. When Maria told Ricardo this batch of biscuits was his best ever, Ricardo spread his hands in the manner of one stating the obvious, and said, 'That's because NOW I have the proper cooking THINGS!'

Laying the table

Most children love laying the table. To start with you can make a drawing on a piece of card to show how to lay out everything just the way you like it. You could even do a life-size card for each person, so the child just has to match each item to the picture, as if it were a place mat.

In the bathroom

Make sure you are up to date with his toilet training progress and have the potty or trainer seat to hand as required. Provide a standing stool in the bathroom so that he can access the toilet, sink, soap, his flannel, and a towel (making sure all medicines, razors and other hazards are out of his reach). Show him how to turn the tap on and off, avoid scalding himself with hot water, and put in or take out the plug. Show him the soap, where it goes, or how to use the dispenser. Show him how you wash your hands and let him demonstrate how he can do the same. Keep a toothbrush and child's toothpaste at your home, and supervise toothbrushing so that he doesn't use too much paste and does a thorough job.

In the living room

Enlist your grandchild's help in plumping up cushions, dusting the television screen and dusting or polishing tables and chairs. If you are vacuuming, let him have a go and he will find it tremendous fun providing he's not frightened by the noise.

In your living room have a big box or basket of toys where your grandchild can get things out without having to ask for help. At the end of the day, help her put everything away. Toys with lots of small pieces, like a farm or train set or jigsaw puzzles, should live in their own boxes. Teach the child that these things should be taken out and played with, and then put away before something else is brought out, otherwise everything could get lost and muddled and won't be fun to play with anymore.

Have a box or shelf with books suitable for her age and encourage her to explore them on her own as well as having you read them out. Show her how to turn pages without tearing them, and how to carry a book without the pages flopping open to protect them from damage.

In the bedrooms

If the child is sleeping over at your home, engage him in helping to keep his room tidy and he can help tuck in sheets and smooth the duvet. Provide a place for his clothes that he can reach and show him how to fold and stack the same kinds of clothes together. When he's getting dressed let the child choose what he wants to wear, but limit the choice to two or three items.

You may prefer to keep your own bedroom as a 'no-go area'.

Meals and snacks

Every generation has its own hang-ups about food. People who can remember going hungry as children, or struggling to feed their own children, have a different relationship with food from people who have never experienced deprivation. For grandparents who have known want, wasting food can feel very wrong.

Changing attitudes to food

These days, parents are likely to be more concerned with protecting their children from the current epidemic of childhood obesity. They may want their child to learn to stop eating when she has had enough, rather than being urged to 'take one more mouthful.' National figures show that one in five reception age children are overweight, rising to one in three by Year 6. In this context, exhortations to 'finish your plate' seem counterproductive. Children who are cared for by their grandparents are more likely to be overweight, so this is an area where we don't necessarily know best.

Follow instructions

When you are in charge of the grandchildren, you can have your own approach to mealtimes, but as with every other aspect of childcare, never undermine or criticise the parents in any way. If you think they are doing something wrong, ask them, out of the child's hearing, what the rationale is behind their approach. If you want them to trust you with their children, respect their instructions about specific foods that are not to be served, whether for reasons of religion, allergies (real or imagined), saving the planet, or protecting the child's teeth. Anyway, it is possible that your ideas are out of line with the latest research in nutrition and that what they are doing is right.

Helen's granddaughter Mimi was adorably chubby as a one-year-old and she enjoyed her food. Helen thought the parents were worrying unnecessarily about the child's weight. When she was asked to look after Mimi one day, they gave her instructions about the quantity the child was allowed to eat. Helen, who had raised three children of her own, thought this was nonsense. In her view, children were the best judge of when they had had enough. It didn't seem right to stop feeding Mimi when she was still opening her mouth for more, so Helen continued to spoon food into her, waiting for some sign that she was full. The sign did not come before Helen lost her nerve and put down the spoon. She finally had to admit that this child really didn't know when to stop.

Cause for concern

There may be situations when you are so sure that the parents' approach to feeding the child is ill-judged and potentially doing harm, that you feel you just have to challenge them. This is serious. Don't try to deal with this with hints and aside comments. Prepare yourself for what will be an uncomfortable conversation that is likely to be resented. Marshall the reasons for your concern, research the facts, talk to someone you trust. When you are ready, and you are sure that this needs to be addressed, broach the matter out of the hearing of the child and in as sympathetic and non-judgemental way as you can, backed up with an offer of help and support.

Maggie's toddler grandson was a 'picky eater' who rarely ate the meals she put before him when the family came to visit. She noticed one day that after he had refused to touch his meal and had got down from the table, Maggie's daughter fed him biscuits from her handbag. She decided to say nothing, but when the same thing happened a few weeks later, she broached the subject with her daughter. It was awkward at first, and her daughter was defensive, but when Maggie shared her own experiences of trying to get her children to eat properly, her daughter was able to share her despair that the child would eat virtually nothing but biscuits. Together they researched how to get expert advice to deal with the situation. Maggie was able to support her daughter through a difficult period as she implemented the recommended solution.

Changing ideas

There have been a few changes in ideas about feeding children over the last few years.

For babies there is no doubt that 'breast is best' and a lot more effort goes into helping new mothers succeed with breastfeeding than used to be the case. If you breastfed your own babies you can be a great additional source of encouragement and personal tips for the new mother. However, mothers who can't or don't want to breastfeed are likely to have had their fill of the 'breast-feeding mafia'. So if the mother has decided not to go down this route, respect her wishes.

You may remember when solid foods used to be started any time from three months. Then, as more was learned about the development of the digestive system, six months became the earliest recommended time. Now the differences among children are recognised and some experts recommend starting on solid foods between four and six months depending on the baby's signs of readiness. Timing the introduction of solids is a decision the parents will probably want to take.

Many parents will be following the 'baby-led weaning' approach, basically putting bits of 'real food' on the highchair tray and letting the child handle it and feed herself. This method skips the purée stage altogether, and many babies do prefer 'real food' food with some texture and taste. Babies left to feed themselves this way seem to enjoy it and have fun squeezing and smearing the food everywhere. Foods that are particular choking hazards should be cut up or not offered. Get the parent to talk you through what they want you to do, and borrow any books they have so you can read what they have been reading.

Another discovery in the last 20 years is that honey can be dangerous for babies in their first year, because it can carry the spores that cause botulism and babies that age do not have the immunity to deal with this.

Food allergies

More children have food allergies these days. Doctors don't understand exactly why, but one theory is that we are too careful about hygiene and don't give children's developing immune systems enough to get their teeth into. Without the traditional 'peck of dirt' to work on, the immune system develops reactions to foods and other environmental allergens instead. There is also an inherited aspect to the tendency, and the children of parents with food allergies are more likely to have allergies too, though not necessarily to the same foods. Around between 5 to 10% of children now have some sort of food allergy or intolerance, so make sure that you know if your grandchildren have any issues.

Severe allergic reactions are uncommon but they are serious. If the doctor has prescribed an epinephrine pen, make sure you are given it when you are looking after the child, and that you understand when and how to use it and what to do next.

Snacks

Little children have little tummies and need feeding mid morning and mid afternoon to keep going between meals. The secret is to make these snacks just as healthy as the main meals, so that if they don't eat much at lunch or dinner, but will eat snacks, it doesn't matter. If they are used to grazing in their own house, and can't go a couple of hours without asking for something, make sure you have a supply of fruit, carrot sticks or non-salty crackers they can eat. If they are not hungry for those things, they are not really hungry at all.

Holly's 'morning snacks' are legendary among her grandchildren. She arranges a selection of berries, apple wedges, nectarine slices, orange segments, banana slices or halved grapes elegantly on a small plate along with a cream cracker or rice cake. As the food is low in fat and quickly digested, Holly is happy to offer 'morning snack' mid-morning and mid-afternoon without worrying that it will spoil the child's appetite for lunch or dinner.

Sweets and chocolate

Sweets and chocolate are a traditional grandparental treat, but they are nutritionally empty, unarguably bad for children's teeth and can be the source of a lot of tiresome pestering if you become known as a soft touch. Don't give sweets to your grandchildren without asking the parents for permission. Of course children should be allowed to enjoy sweets from time to time, but they should not be a daily treat, and the parents would probably prefer to be the ones to indulge them.

Fat, salt and sugar

In developed countries, the main problem with children's eating habits is that they eat too much fat, salt and sugar. Fats are high calorie, but at least they carry important nutrients and lead to a feeling of fullness. Salt makes children thirsty and if they won't drink water it leads to taking in extra calories in drinks. It is also bad for the kidneys and associated with high blood pressure. Sugar provides instant energy but leads to an energy dip an hour or so later and a craving for more, and is probably what lies behind the current epidemic of obesity and diabetes. And it really does rot the teeth, for which they won't thank you when they get older. Cakes and biscuits should be a treat, not part of the daily snack routine.

Martha enjoys looking after her grandchildren and when they come to stay she likes to take them shopping to choose what they will all have to eat for lunch. If they ask for junk food or sweets, she just says, 'Grandma doesn't buy those things'. She then goes on to explain why not and what foods she does buy. The grandchildren soon learn that she is firm about this and stop even bothering to ask.

Drinks

Fruit juice used to be considered a healthy drink for children, now not so much, even if it is pure fruit and unsweetened. Fruit juices are bad for teeth because of their acidity as well as their natural fruit sugar content and they contain calories the child may not need if he is just thirsty. These days, tap water is considered the drink of choice for quenching thirst, and children should have ready access to it through the day. Milk is important but should be seen as a food rather than a thirst-quencher. Get full fat milk for children, they need the nutrients that skimming removes. Fruit juice should be limited to one beaker a day, and fizzy sugary drinks should not be an option at all.

Healthy eating and variety

Research has shown that the appetite is stimulated when a variety of foods is provided. Think of buffets at holiday hotels and how everyone loads their plates with a bit of this and a bit of that. Laboratory rats get fat if, after they have had enough of one food, a different one is offered. You can use that knowledge when preparing food for your grandchildren. They will probably eat more vegetables, for example, if they are served small portions of two or three varieties than if they are given a big helping of just one kind.

Offering a small portion of vegetable as a separate starter course is another strategy worth trying. Children are more likely to eat it when they are at their hungriest. But don't make an issue of it if they don't want it this time, and just go on to the main course.

Stelios usually prepares lunch while his wife takes the grandchildren to the park. His speciality is a vegetable meze. He lightly cooks a variety of vegetables and offers them, cut up, in little bowls. The variety usually includes baby carrots or carrot sticks, baby corn, green beans, broccoli or cauliflower florets and courgette sticks. The children select one or two from each bowl and are allowed to eat them with their fingers, dipping the vegetables into a choice of hummus or tzatziki. With their appetites sharpened by a run in the playground, the challenge of getting the dip to stick to the vegetables, and the variety of taste and texture combinations on offer, this is a favourite with the children.

Avoiding mealtime battles

Children have a strong need for independence and for exerting some kind of control on their environment. Refusing to eat what is provided, demanding certain foods, or deciding when they will eat are all ways they can do this. They also have a strong need for attention, and if playing up at mealtimes is a good way of getting this, play up they will! As a grandparent, the chances are that they will be as good as gold when you are presiding over the table. This is because they are likely to be more wary of entering into a battle of wills with you than with their parents, and less interested in winning. However, your grandchild may be the exception. These strategies have worked in our families and are worth a try.

Engage the child in meal planning, shopping and preparation

Make meal planning part of the structure of your day, discussing with children what they would like to eat, and offering options that you are equally happy about providing. The smaller the child, the fewer the options they should be offered, so toddlers should be offered two choices, rather than the open-ended, 'What shall we have for lunch?' Children usually love to help you prepare meals, pouring pasta into a measuring cup, washing vegetables or counting out berries onto dessert plates. All this makes them mindful of what they are eating and gives them a sense of having some control over it without having to make a scene.

Respect their preferences and work round them

We all have likes and dislikes. Children's preferences often change from week to week, (unless of course some adult fixes the idea by stating that 'Billy doesn't like fish' in his hearing) so just offer a small portion of a previously rejected food from time to time and don't draw attention to it.

Make meal times social occasions

Children enjoy rituals and ceremony. They enjoy laying the table and pointing out that 'Grandad sits here, and Granny sits there, and I sit here'. They enjoy meal-time conversation, as long as it involves them and isn't about what they are not eating. A good conversational gambit is going over what you did together all morning and what you are planning to do all afternoon.

4

Make sure the child is hungry by lunchtime

Stick to her regular snack and meal-times, the same time as at nursery or at home, which is when her body will be ready for something. If you offer the child a healthy mid-morning snack, she should be hungry for lunch two hours later. If she isn't, she may not have had enough exercise. A run in the park before lunch is a great aid to appetite. But it is also true that some days, small children just don't seem to want to eat much, and that is OK too.

5

Offer small portions

It is much better for your morale and that of the child if she asks for seconds rather than pushing away a half-finished plate. Children can't eat much at a sitting so offer her a bit less than you think she needs and let her decide to come back for more.

6

Don't make a big deal about dessert

Fruits or yoghurts are good everyday desserts, and there is no reason to deny the child these even if they didn't feel like finishing their main course. It is fine to serve something a bit sweeter or richer from time to time, but don't build dessert up as the high point of the meal. If you have had a cooking session in the morning, serve the cupcakes or gingerbread men you made as a dessert rather than letting the child eat them as soon as they have cooled. Pack up a selection for the child to take home to share with his family.

7

Be a good role model

Just as the child will copy the way you handle your knife and fork, she will copy your eating habits and your table manners. If the child is not allowed a book or a toy at table, you are not allowed your mobile phone or newspaper.

8

Show interest in what the child does eat

Children crave attention, so pay attention to what he does eat and talk about why it tastes good and how it is good for him. Don't over-promise on the benefits though.

Freddy was clearly not happy as he sat glowering at his plate. 'What is the matter, sweetheart?' asked his grandmother. 'You said if I ate my dinners all up I'd get big and strong like Daddy. Well, I ATE my dinners all up. And I'm NOT big and strong like Daddy!'

Rainy days

What can you do to entertain a small child on a day when it is forecast to rain all day long?

First of all, do get the child out of the house for some fresh air at some stage. Getting the wellies and raincoats on and going for a stamp and splash in puddles can be a lot of fun. It helps to keep spare socks and trousers or tights for the child to change into on your return – some water is bound to splash in over the boots. However, even after an exhilarating outing like that, you will still be left with a lot of day to get through. It is worth planning how to fill it enjoyably.

Here are some games that have made rainy days special in our families, and have been played over and over again. They all help develop the child's creative imagination, encourage exploration and problem-solving, and provide lots of opportunities for talking about the child's own experiences, likes and dislikes and rehearsing social occasions. They work well with one child and are even more fun with two or three.

Adapt these games to move at the rate that is comfortable for the child. Younger children, or those with special needs, may be overwhelmed by too much detail. Keep it simple and add detail when they have processed the experience and are ready for more. Children with vivid imaginations will want to take over the story: that's fine, encourage them. More practical children will want to push the pace and get straight to the action, that's fine too. Let the child dictate the pace and direction of the game.

Step back as soon as any element of the game has captured the child's imagination and he is playing independently. Step in again with the next element of the game, or with a different activity, as soon as independent play is starting to pall. If he isn't interested at all, just leave the game for another day.

Teddy's birthday

This is a tried and tested favourite which can be adapted to suit two to five year-olds and is brilliant fun! It can last as a running theme all day with breaks for meals and doing other things. Don't push it if the child loses interest, just do something else and come back to it later. Don't move on to the next step if the child becomes absorbed in any aspect and is happy playing on his own for a bit. It doesn't matter if you skip some bits and cut straight to the finale.

You will need:

- a favourite teddy or doll and a few other soft toys
- paper and crayons
- wrapping paper
- sticky tape or a glue stick
- balloons
- a few stickers
- snack food such as raisins, small crackers, cubes of cheese
- a cupcake
- two or three birthday candles.

What you do:

Announce that it is Teddy's birthday today and he's having a party!

Who's coming? Ask the child to decide which five or six toys are to be invited and where they live (for older children encourage this to be as widely distributed around your home as possible).

Cut invitation cards out of a sheet of paper and get the child to decorate them. Has he ever had an invitation? Did he make invitations for his birthday, or did Mummy buy them?

- Put the cards in a bag and let the child play postman delivering them to each toy in their home. What did they say? Can they come?

- Presents! Help the child find small items for presents, one for each guest to give. What would Teddy like? Some crayons? A toy car?

- Provide some big squares of used wrapping paper and strips of sticky tape or a glue stick for the child to wrap the gifts with. Stand by to help out and make sure they won't come apart in the post.

- Ask the child to distribute the wrapped presents to the guests, and to tell them not to open them, they are for Teddy!

- What's for tea? Draw circles on a plain piece of paper and ask the child to draw pizzas or cakes on them, cut them out and put the paper food on small saucers or plates.

- Blow up some balloons and ask the child to decorate the party area. Yes, he can play with them first, but try not to pop them before the party. (Don't let under-threes play with popped or deflated balloons.)

- Party-time! Ask the child to collect the guests and their presents and line them up outside the party area. No pushing or shoving!

- When they are satisfactorily arranged, ask the child to help Teddy invite them in. Join in the fun by voicing the guests as the presents are handed over and opened. Sadly, not all the toys are well-behaved...

- Put on some music and help the child engage the toys in musical bumps, statues etc. Have toy races and award stickers to the winning toys as prizes 1st, 2nd and 3rd. Comfort the losers.

- Announce time for party tea and get the child to sit the toys in a circle round the paper food. Provide a plate of (carpet-friendly) real snack food for the child to share with the toys.

- The finale! Come in singing Happy Birthday, with a surprise real cupcake with two or three candles on and let the child help Teddy blow them out and eat the cake.

Going on holiday

This is infinitely adaptable, depending on the child's experience of holidays and the props you happen to have around. You will need paper and crayons and a cardboard box big enough to sit a few toys in.

- Tell the child that the toys are going on holiday! Has she ever been on a holiday? Where did she go? What did she like about it? What kind of holiday would the toys like best? The seaside?

- Where shall we go? Help the child choose somewhere away from the usual play area to be the holiday destination and place a few simple props to indicate the kind of holiday it is to be. The seaside could be indicated by a bit of blue cloth and some shells, or you could ask the child to draw a picture. The point of the game is the journey to get there.

- Now ask the child to decide who is coming and make sure they all have a good sleep now because they are going on a long journey tomorrow. Younger children will have fun settling the toys to sleep.

- While the toys have a sleep, help the child to prepare the things the toys will need on holiday. This can range from an imaginary list to real props. Pre-schoolers will enjoy drawing and cutting out things to pack. The cardboard box will need decorating with big black wheels if it is a car or bus, blue waves if is a ferry and so on. Older children could draw a map. You could even make small suitcases out of folded card and sticky tape if you are feeling really creative.

- Wake-up time! Everybody up, time to go on holiday!

- The toys pile in the cardboard box and set off on their long and eventful journey, probably without too much further intervention from you other than providing the odd sign, obstruction, or roadside café.

Racetrack!

This is a variant on the 'marble run' idea with the advantage of not needing marbles, making it safe for under-threes. It will entertain car-lovers for hours.

You will need:

- a few toy cars
- a few cardboard boxes
- strong scissors and lots of broad sticky tape
- a measuring tape and string are optional extras.

What you do

- The idea is to create a ramp down which a toy car will run at exciting speed without falling off or turning over when it hits the floor. Wooden floors work better than carpet, which will require bigger cars to cope with the resistance of the pile.

- Start modestly with one box, using a flap cut off from the long side and taped to the upside down box as a ramp.

- Engage the child in your planning and trial runs. Talk about how things don't always work first time, and the importance of trial and error.

- Talk about the science of what you are doing in simple language. Talk about the ramp being too steep or the carpet too bumpy. You could even show him what an angle is and talk about the angle between the ramp and floor or the ramp and the platform being too big or too small.

- Build on success by raising the first box onto a second box, and adding to the ramp. This gets tricky! Talk about the problems and ask him to help you work out what to do.

- Make sure the child can reach high enough to start the car down the track by himself.

- The satisfaction comes from the combination of speed and a smooth landing, so don't over-complicate the track.

- Be a model of patience and persistence yourself, but talk about what it feels like when things don't work the way you want them to. Does that sometimes happen to him? How does he feel?

- Stretch a bit of string to make a finish line and see which car gets closest. You could show him how to use a measuring tape for accuracy. Award 1st, 2nd, 3rd place to the ones that go farthest.

Toy school

The game is that the toys are starting school, and the child will be the teacher. This is a winner for pre-school children who will be starting school themselves soon and will welcome an opportunity to rehearse what it will be like and talk about any anxieties.

You will need:

- some teddies or dolls
- a big piece of material for cutting up (an old plain-coloured skirt or shirt would be fine)
- measuring tape
- some ribbon
- scissors
- paper and pencils
- old magazines
- a stapler (optional).

What you do:

- First the toys will need their school uniforms. Ask the child to help you measure one of the toys across the tummy (width) and from neck to knees (length). Cut a rectangle out of the material of the measured width and twice the length. Cut a sideways slit in the middle for the head, and enlarge it with another slit at right angles, from the centre of the first cut, until the hole will fit teddy's big head. Tie a bit of ribbon round teddy's tummy for a belt. Now do the same for the other toys. There is no need for stitching, the tabards will look wonderful just like that.

- Ask the child to find a suitable place for the school and help her prop the toys up against the furniture.

- Teacher will need a register! Write the names of the toys on a piece of paper with boxes for the child to tick and ask her to tick them off if they are present.

- While the child is doing this, make some toy books out of the old magazines by cutting rectangles from the spines, each including a staple. You can make blank books with plain paper and a stapler. Don't make them too thick or they won't close.

- Playtime! A chair can be a climbing frame for the toys.

- Dinner! Make a yummy school dinner with paper plates and pretend food.

- Singing and story time! You could join in.

- Toy school can turn into a running game. Keep your eye out for miniature props. Maybe even make little schoolbags and fill them with little books and cut down crayons, ready for the next rainy day.

Rainy day drawer

Meera has a drawer under her bed, hidden from view by the bedspread. She uses this as her 'rainy day drawer' for when she has the grandchildren for the day and it is too wet for the park. Whenever she passes a market stall, goes to a fête, or spots a book sale, she looks out for things to put in it. Small novelties, puzzles, sticker books and unusual arts and crafts materials go in there, to be produced when some extra stimulus is needed to help get to the end of a long day.

Treasure Island

This game is all about detective work with the goal of finding where you have hidden a treasure chest. It works well with children from around the age of three, and is more fun with more than one child.

You will need:

- any kind of ornate box or decorated gift box
- some old costume jewellery
- some kind of small treat or novelty for each child eg a brownie wrapped in foil or a sheet of stickers
- paper and pencil.

It is fun to get this ready in advance, but be prepared to have to run it again, with fresh clues (and another treat).

What you do:

- Fill the box with the jewellery, and a treat or novelty for each child.
- Hide the box.
- Make a list of the places to hide your clues. The older the child, the more clues will be needed, but anywhere between four and eight clues usually works.

- Think of a clue for each hiding place. It could be a picture, a word, or a rhyming riddle, depending on the age of the child. Don't make them too hard the first time.

- If you have more than one child in the game, give each child a chance to have a clue just for them, so that the oldest doesn't have all the fun. Fold over the paper and write the relevant child's name on the front.

- Number the clues and plant them working backwards from the treasure.

- Make a realistic treasure map of an island with 'x' marks the spot, add a hint about where to find the first clue, dab the paper all over with a wet teabag, cut around the edges to make them irregular, and scrunch it up.

- As soon as the map is dry, give it to the oldest child - you are ready to start the treasure hunt.

Rainy day rituals

Children love rituals and will quickly turn something that was supposed to happen 'just this once' into a regular expectation. So if you decide on some normally forbidden treat because it is so wet, be prepared for an expectant face next time it rains. Children's memory for special treats is long and tenacious. That said, establishing a ritual of doing something special is an excellent way of brightening a dull day. Useful rainy day rituals could include a trip to a shopping mall with a small sum to spend; a trip to a café for lunch; a visit to the library; a museum visit; making flapjacks; arts and crafts with special rainy day glitter pens and so on.

A bedroom for toy people, a jungle, a prehistoric landscape for dinosaurs or a space scene can all be made quite easily by covering the inside of the box with a painted backdrop or gluing on wrapping paper (for wallpaper) or cut-out pictures from magazines or holiday brochures. When the backdrop is finished to the child's satisfaction, you add the props. These could be as simple as pictures drawn or glued on stiff card and stood on blobs of Plasticine. Matchboxes make great beds, or chests of drawers, or television sets. Bits cut from egg-boxes make a magnificent moonscape, or a row of volcanoes. You could even try your hand at a bit of papier mache modelling, using strips of newspaper and PVA glue diluted 50:50 with water.

For a more dramatic effect, although with less play potential, leave the box whole, apart from the flaps, and suspend items from the 'roof' with thread. That way you can make an aquarium, a butterfly house or a space scene with planets.

Dioramas

A great project for pre-schoolers is making a diorama (a three-dimensional scene). That sounds grand enough to be intriguing, but only needs a cardboard box with the flaps and one side cut away. The idea is to create a scene on the three remaining sides with the bottom acting as the stage on which you put moveable props and characters, like little people or animals from the toy box. The more the child helps you design and execute the project, the more their imagination will come into play and the less critical they will be of the outcome. It is the process of making it which provides most of the fun.

Liz had great success with a Narnian scene, using cut up Christmas cards to make the backdrop of snowy trees, gluing cotton wool on the ground for snow, and putting a lamp-post made from a pencil and some Plasticine in the centre. She painted a big wardrobe on one of the discarded bits of cardboard and cut it to make the doors open and shut. Then she taped the cardboard to the front of the diorama on one side, so that it could be opened out to magically reveal the winter scene inside. The little girls played Narnia all afternoon, and insisted on taking the whole thing home with them at the end of the day.

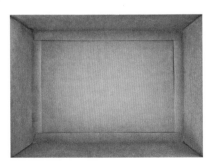

Days out

Going off on an adventure together will be fun for everyone, and lots of enjoyable expeditions can be organised more or less for free. Others cost money but are worth it from time to time, as special occasion treats. Don't raise the bar too high too quickly: a trip to Legoland or Alton Towers will set a standard of excitement against which the local canal museum will not easily compete.

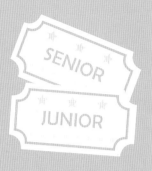

SENIOR

JUNIOR

Jean felt that with having a full-time job and elderly parents to look after, she really could not take on any kind of childcare. However, she loved to take her grandchildren out, one at a time, for special trips that the parents were unlikely to arrange. She saw herself as a 'giant playmate' with special resources at her disposal, and the grandchildren enjoyed some memorable days with her.

Local treasures

Much depends on where you live. If you are in easy reach of the sea, skip the rest of this chapter: a day at the beach is child heaven. If you are in easy reach of a zoo, theme park, or safari park, see if you can buy an annual ticket that gives unlimited entry. Join the National Trust if there are Trust properties in easy reach as this will enable you to go back time and time again.

Gloria and Stephen live in Warwickshire, near Mary Arden's house and a working Tudor farm. They have a family membership and every time the grandchildren come up from London for the weekend they make at least one trip to see the pigs and chickens, goats and sheep, owls and falcons. There are always new animals to meet and new things going on. To little city-dwellers, the sight of a cow being milked or pigs being fed is just as exotic as a trip to the zoo.

A good start for getting ideas for other local outings is the internet. Search 'things to do with children' and wherever it is you live. You may be surprised at the number of adventure playgrounds or soft play centres there are around and you may find special events for children that are laid on for free. School or church fêtes, fairs and puppet shows are other things to look out for. Even a garden centre can make a good outing, especially if they have a fish tank or a play area.

For toddlers a good outing can be as simple as exploring a woodland, finding a stream for playing Pooh sticks with you, or going to a canal to watch the boats go through the locks. Older children will enjoy going for a walk they have not been on before, especially if there is something of interest to aim for. A view, a river, a playground or a railway bridge all make good destinations. Just make sure the child is wearing comfortable shoes, you are carrying protection against the elements for both of you, and you have packed the picnic without which the outing will fall flat!

Don has a grandson with attention deficit and hyperactivity. 'Max is fine with me. I organise to do things with him all day, mostly out of the house. No watching telly, no telling him to go and play with toys. He isn't picky about what we do, and we have some good little chats as we go along. I like the feeling we have a special relationship, Max and me.'

Library

A trip to the library makes a good outing for story-lovers. There may be a weekly story-time laid on, with a box of toys brought out at the end. Even if not, just letting the child discover interesting-looking books and bring them to you for reading there and then can occupy up to an hour. Then there is the whole ritual of choosing books to take home. Sign up the child with his own membership card so he can make his own choices. If you are late returning the books the fines for late return also tend to be less punitive for children than adults.

Leisure centres

Get onto the website of your local leisure centre and see what activities are provided for children. Learning any kind of physical skill gives a child self-confidence and she might discover an activity for which she'll develop a lasting interest. Find out when children can use the swimming pool. Maybe you could even teach her to swim! While you are there, see if you can get some exercise time in yourself. Some leisure centres run a crèche where, for a small fee, you can leave a child half an hour or so in safe hands, while you go for a swim or hit the gym. Check with the parents whether they would be happy with such an arrangement before trying it out.

The country hotel near Joan's house has a spa and swimming pool. As she was a member herself she negotiated with the management for a special deal that allows her grandchildren to use these facilities whenever they come to stay for the weekend.

Museums

Museums in the UK are often free and can make enjoyable outings for even the youngest of children – provided you follow a few basic rules.

1 Do your homework

Check on the museum website what is laid on for families with children and what they have that is likely to interest your grandchild. Museum websites will guide you to the items of most interest to children so you can plan your visit before you leave home. There may be child-friendly maps, puzzles or a checklist of things to spot or count or other special facilities for children so make sure you ask at the desk when you arrive. Some museums or galleries lay on activity sessions for children, when they can make things related to the theme of the exhibitions, but you usually have to book places in advance.

2 Prepare the child

Once you know what is there and have decided what you are going to see, whet the child's appetite with stories or discussions related to the exhibits.

> On the way to the transport museum, Grandpa explained to three-year-old Noah that they would be seeing all kinds of trains and buses, but that they would be standing still, they wouldn't be moving. 'I know THAT,' said Noah, who had been to a museum before. 'It's because they are all dead'.

3 Pack snacks and drinks

That way you can choose whether or not to visit the café. You don't want to be forced to join a queue if it's busy, and looking at exhibits is hungry and thirsty work.

4 Announce the destination with confidence

Don't say, 'Would you like to go to the Heritage museum or watch TV?' but, 'We are going to see how Grandad's mummy used to live!'

5 Get there early

If the destination is at all popular it is well worthwhile getting there ten minutes before opening time. When you get inside, go straight for the most popular attraction first as the queue to see it will only get worse. Most tourist attractions are busiest between 11 am and 4 pm, because of people coming from afar.

6 Keep the visit focused

Plan to do just one topic or one room. Leave the children wanting more.

7 Keep the visit short.

Don't expect to spend much more than 30 minutes looking at exhibits with a child who is under five-years-old.

8 Follow the child's interests

If she is fascinated by the first thing you come to, don't hurry her along, even if it is only the donations box that has grabbed her attention. What she has spotted may be more interesting to her than what you had planned, and it is all good learning. You can always come back if you don't see all you wanted.

> Deepa took her little grandson into the city to visit a special exhibition at the museum. When she brought him home, he raced into the house shouting, 'Mummy, Mummy, I rode on an escalator!'

Art galleries

Art galleries have most appeal for small children if you forget about 'art' and 'artists' and just go to look carefully at one or two interesting pictures. Get the child to spot things and talk about what he has seen, just as you would with a picture in a book. A great introduction to art galleries are the books by James Mayhew about Katie and her grandmother (such as *Katie and the British Artists* published by Orchard) in which a little girl pops in and out of famous pictures, making friends with the characters. It would be exciting for a child to recognise one of the pictures in those books as you walked through the gallery.

Gift shops

You may as well accept that all museums, galleries, zoos, theme parks and stately homes will route you through their gift shop on the way out. You can buy some wonderfully educational books and games in these places, as well as a lot of over-priced souvenirs that your grandchild will go straight towards. It is best to have a consistent policy, to avoid whining. You can just say, 'No, Nana doesn't buy those things. She buys you presents at Christmas and birthdays'. As long as you are consistent, this will work, and it makes such trips more affordable. Alternatively, you could set the child a price limit and show him what sort of item that means. The advantage of allowing the child to choose a gift is that it makes the idea of a trip like this more appealing next time. Reframe the purchase in your own mind as a donation to the museum.

If he doesn't see anything he wants within your limit, your generous offer can turn into a tragedy. Some compensation for the disappointment is fair, perhaps in the shape of an ice lolly, but don't up your limit to pacify him. Next time you can simply sweep through the shop saying, 'You don't like any of those things, remember?'

Visiting friends and family

If there is an elderly friend or relative that you visit, take along your grandchild once in a while. This can make an outing for the child and give a lot of pleasure to the old person. You will want to let the parents know in advance what the plan is, especially if the old person has had a stroke or is obviously unwell. They can help you prepare the child, explaining for example, 'Auntie Dorothy's not very well so she has to stay in bed. But she can talk to people and she would like to meet you.' Help the child to make a gift of some sort, maybe

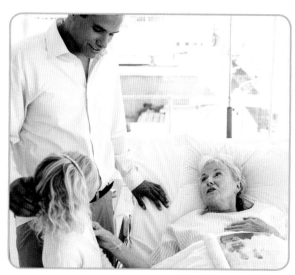

a drawing or some cupcakes. Offering these will make him feel important and generous, and provide an opening for the old person to engage him in conversation. Take along a few toys or a sticker book to keep him entertained when the conversation palls, and don't stay too long. It is good for children to get to know elderly people and to understand the whole cycle of life. There will probably be a few questions later about getting old and dying, so check with the parents how they want you to handle these should they arise.

Retaining the learning

The child will have learned a lot on your outing, so make sure the learning sticks by referring back to the trip. Talk about what you have seen together, get the child to draw a picture of something he saw for Mummy and Daddy, and text the parents with a brief resume of the day so they know what to ask about. You could make a scrapbook with photos from the day and pictures or maps out of brochures. A few days later, introduce that educational book or game you picked up at the shop while the child was choosing his souvenir.

Travelling with children

Whatever kind of outing you go on, there is bound to be some waiting around: for the bus, in a queue or to be served. This is something the children will hate even more than you do. You will probably remember the strategies you used with your own children in these circumstances, 'I spy' being the perennial favourite. Here are some other useful ones along the same lines.

Waiting around

The humming game

Everyone takes turns to hum a well-known tune and the others have to try and guess what it is. If anyone gets it right, praise goes to both guesser and hummer.

The silence game

This one is especially good for waiting to be served in cafés when the children are getting noisy and you are getting embarrassed. The game is that the first one to speak or laugh out loud is out. Everyone has to try to make the others speak or laugh without doing it themselves. The good thing about this game is that the youngest child is often the one to hold out longest.

The picnic game

You start by saying, *'Teddy had a picnic and he brought one jam sandwich'*. The next person says, *'Teddy had a picnic and he brought one jam sandwich and two smelly socks'*, or whatever. And so it goes on, everyone adding something and the first person to forget something on the list being out. Grandparents are not very good at this game and usually lose, to the delight of the children!

The choosing game

This goes, '*If you could have any of those shops/cars/fairground rides/zoo animals/pet (or whatever suits the circumstances) what one would you choose?*' They have to make a choice and then say what would be good about their choice, and maybe what would be not so good. To make it fun, you have to join in with your choices and your reasons, whether serious or played for laughs.

Rigmarole

This one is best for car journeys as it can go on and on. One person starts, '*Once upon a time...*' and starts making up a story. After a bit, preferably at an exciting moment rather than waiting for invention to flag, you interrupt and name another person to pick up the story. Once they get used to it, they will hand the baton on themselves. All contributions are taken seriously and woven into the story, with you taking responsibility for making sure the youngest child's ideas are developed and that all plot strands are resolved at the end.

In-car entertainment

Songs or stories for young children played on the car CD player are usually appreciated and there are plenty of compilations to choose from. A small selection is enough as children enjoy familiarity, especially if it is hard to hear on a motorway.

Sing-alongs and story-telling

You can be the in-car entertainment all by yourself. Young children love hearing you talk and sing to them. Even if they don't join in the sing-along, they may like to choose which song you should sing next.

Jay was driving his baby granddaughter Naila home. She was just learning to talk and 'More!' was her only word so far. To pass the time on the journey, Jay reminded her about all the things she had done with her grandparents that day from the moment she had arrived. When he had finished, there was silence. Then a little voice at the back of the car said, 'More?' So Jay started all over again.

Car safety

There are regulations about restraining children in cars. By law, the responsibility lies with the driver of the car, so make sure you are familiar with the regulations. It is your responsibility to make sure the child is properly fastened into the correct child restraint before you set off on your journey, however short. If you are travelling in a taxi or hire car, ask if they can provide the appropriate seats. If a child restraint is not available, a child may travel unrestrained in a licensed taxi or licensed hire car. This is not because it is safe, it is just for reasons of practicality.

If you are driving, make sure you have the correct car seats for the age and size of the child. If the parents are dropping the child off by car, get them to leave you their seat, and make sure you know how to fix it in place in your car and strap in the child. Some of the designs are counter-intuitive and fiendish to work out so don't be content with watching a demonstration. Make sure you can do it 'all by yourself' before the parent leaves for the day. If you will be driving your grandchild a lot it may be worth investing in a seat of your own. It will need replacing as the child grows, and you can't get them second-hand in case they have been damaged in an accident. Never carry children in the front seat, especially not if your car has passenger airbags.

If no child seat is available, the child must use the adult belt instead. A study of car accidents involving children showed that grandparents are more likely to be carrying young children unrestrained than parents are. Maybe this is because of having cars without the latest safety gear, or maybe it is because of failure to catch up with modern attitudes to restraining children in cars. Either way, don't add to those statistics. Toddlers may furiously object to being strapped in, but this is one of those occasions when there can be no compromise. No strap, no trip.

When Eileen's children were little they had several glorious holidays with their relatives in the West of Ireland. For trips to the seaside, the back seat of the station wagon was folded down and six or seven children piled in with their buckets and spades. She reminded her son of this when he was giving her a demonstration of how to fix the car seats and do up the belts for her little grandchildren, coming to stay for a weekend. Instead of laughing and enjoying the memory, he got quite angry about the fact that she had taken risks all those years ago.

Holidays

Grandparents assume a special importance when it comes to holiday time, even if they don't have that much contact the rest of the year. Chances are that if you have school-aged grandchildren, you will be roped in to look after them for at least some of the school holidays.

A recent UK survey showed that a third of grandparents look after their grandchildren more than three times a week during the summer holidays. Nearly half of UK grandparents pay for a family holiday in the first five years after the grandchildren were born. Others help by coming along and acting as chief cook, bottle-washer and babysitter.

The extent to which you want to get involved will depend on the other demands on your time and money, and how much you see the grandchildren during the rest of the year. Sharing a holiday with children and grandchildren can be a very special and rewarding time, or an exhausting experience from which you need a holiday to recover! It can sometimes lead to hurt feelings and resentment that linger on long after the event. Here are some tips we have learned along the way that should make sure it works out for everyone.

Hilda and Spike had 18 grandchildren in five families on two continents. They kept in touch with them while they grew up by renting a house for a month in the summer every year, alternating the continents. The houses were always big rambling places by the sea or on a lake with lots for children to do. Families would come for two or three weeks, variously overlapping so that the cousins all got to know each other as well as each child developing their own special relationship with Granny and Grandad.

Be clear who pays for what and who does what

Clarity is as important as generosity. For example, if you are inviting the family to a house abroad and planning to pay for it, be precise about what it is you will be paying for and what they will need to finance themselves. Will you expect them to pay for their own travel? Will they need to hire a car when they get there? Will everyone be expected to chip in with the shopping? Who will cook? It may feel awkward to get into that sort of detail, but it won't be anything like as awkward as for one or other party to end up having to pay for more than they had bargained for, or do more work than they had anticipated.

Colin's parents run a guesthouse in the Lake District. He was delighted when they invited him and his family to stay for a week in the summer, and had a vision of going off on long walks with his wife while his parents looked after the two little boys. He hadn't reckoned on his parents being fully engaged with looking after the other guests all day and exhausted by the evening. He ended up helping them with their work while his wife got the children out of everyone's way. Further invitations were politely refused.

Alternatively, the parents may invite you to come on holiday with them but don't take that as an indication that they will be paying for everything. Again clarify in advance what it does mean. The simplest way is to ask straight out what your share will cost, giving them the opportunity to make it clear what contribution is expected. Check on travel costs too and if it amounts to more than you are willing to spend, you have the opportunity to bow out in good time and not accept the invitation.

Beryl was in her seventies and widowed, so the invitation to share a rented holiday home with her son and his young family was appealing. She was not in a position to contribute financially, but her offer to babysit every night of the holiday was well-received. In fact, after a day watching three small children run about she was ready for a peaceful evening, and the parents enjoyed their nights out together without feeling guilty.

If you are still at work, or having a busy 'retirement,' you will need a holiday to relax and unwind. Sharing it with the family may not be your idea of fun, in which case bow out gracefully. What you can't do, as a fit adult, is behave like a guest and let the rest of the family do all the work while you put your feet up, whoever is paying. A resort hotel might work better if you are torn between the desire to spend time with the family and your own need to sleep late and lounge by a pool.

Multi-family holidays

If you have more than one child with children of their own it can be wonderful to organise a multi-family holiday where the cousins can get to know each other, and you have all the pleasure of having your whole family around you. Cousins are generally more exciting than siblings and holidays like this cement relationships that can endure for a life-time. Even if no two cousins are the same age, living for a while with a mixed age group of children is a big development experience, a taste of what it is like to grow up in a large family. The older ones learn kindness and responsibility and the younger ones usually repay with adulation.

> Ines and Gabriel had a consistent philosophy about family holidays, so everyone always knew what to expect and what they should contribute. Gabriel paid for the holiday house, and everyone looked after their own travel and car hire. He shopped for basic food and left the other adults to buy in drinks, treats and fancy ingredients. Ines made a simple child-friendly lunch for everyone every day, and left all other meals to the families to sort out amongst themselves. Washing up and any other cleaning needed were down to the families, because Ines would be at her easel. She was always happy to talk to grandchildren while she painted, and even to set them up to paint or draw alongside her, but she didn't undertake to 'mind' them unless they were already asleep.

There are quite a few things to take into account in organising a multi-family holiday, so you have to start planning many months ahead: Christmas is the latest for planning a summer holiday unless you want to find your first choices booked up. You want everyone to enjoy it, so get a few 'musts' and 'must nots' from the potential participants.

If any of the families have school-age children, it must fall in the school holidays. May half-term might be a more affordable option than July or August, provided the grandchildren's half terms all happen at the same time. July and August are not great times to go to places which get hot or bug infested in the summer.

For some families, proximity of amusement parks will rank high, for others it will be cultural sites to visit. A holiday without water involved may be unthinkable for some, and one without good places to eat would disappoint others. You can't please everyone, but you can consult, research and come up with options.

These are some features we would consider essential in a multi-family holiday house:

- double beds for all the adult couples
- one bathroom per family
- a table everyone can sit around to eat, including the children
- a dishwasher and a washing machine
- a living room with comfortable seating for all the adults
- somewhere for children to play indoors without being underfoot
- somewhere for children to play outside without being closely supervised
- easy access to a pool, lake or beach
- shops within a 30 minute drive.

If there are teenagers involved, then everyone's enjoyment will depend on there being enough things for them to do and other teenagers to hang out with. A resort hotel with pools and a disco may be the answer, offering lots for every age group. If it is all-inclusive, that will deal with teenage appetites and endless demands for cold drinks and ice creams, and at least everyone will know up-front what it will cost.

Buying things for your grandchildren

It is great fun choosing presents for grandchildren, and wonderfully satisfying when you get it just right and your present is the one they like best of all. Of course the downside to having that kind of success at birthday or Christmas time is that your gift might eclipse that of the parents or the other grandparents. If your success owes anything to the amount of money you are prepared to spend, they may feel resentful. Buying presents isn't a competition and you don't want to delight your grandchildren at the expense of family harmony. Here are some ways to make sure your gifts are well received by all concerned.

Be sensitive to parent's wishes

No surprises

Children love surprises, their parents not so much – especially if the surprise is bulky, noisy, cuts across their values or is likely to create sibling quarrels. It's much better to ask the parents what would be a good gift, giving them an idea how much you would like to spend. Admittedly, it isn't much fun being asked to buy extra track rather than a new engine, or play food rather than a tea-set, but if that is what is needed it will be appreciated. If you can afford it, by all means offer to buy a big item, like a doll's house or a bike. But check first whether this would be well received and if so whether the parents would prefer to choose the model themselves.

Some of your children may be financially better off than others but don't be tempted to redress the balance through the gifts you give the grandchildren. Sooner or later any special treatment will come out and it is likely to be resented by everyone, winners as well as losers. It's much better to treat all the grandchildren the same. Try not to give young children in the same family presents that are widely different in size, even if they do cost the same. If you give money it's alright to give more to older children, as long as there is some kind of formula so that the younger ones know they will get the same when they are that age.

Parents are likely to be sensitive to any suggestion of criticism behind a gift. So for example, if they are not church-goers, ask before providing the child with a bible, however beautifully illustrated it is. A child's cooking set won't go down well if the parents are already conscious that they make do with too many ready-meals and take-aways. That goes for the children too – a pretty dress doesn't make a good present for the tomboy who likes to live in jeans and a puzzle that is too hard may make a child feel he is not living up to expectations. One that is too easy is just insulting.

Respect the family's values

Of course, no modern grandparent would make the mistake of offering toy guns as a gift. But where do the parents stand on outfits for pirates or knights, complete with foam cutlasses or wooden swords? What about Barbie dolls? You or your children may have loved them, but attitudes have changed and there is now more awareness of the damage that unrealistic or sexualised role models can do. And what about looking after the planet? That plastic climbing frame may delight your toddler grandchild but disturb his environmentally aware parents.

A gift is a gift

Having been handed over, you must never ask what became of your gift. There is nothing more burdensome than an unwanted gift that can't be wrapped up and passed on as a present to someone else because Grandad might find out and be offended. Nor do you really want to extract the confession that little Joey broke it on Christmas morning, or that the parents had to remove the batteries before they were sent distracted and after that it was no fun.

Collectibles

Dolls, teddies and cuddly animals are much loved but too many can be suffocating. Most children choose a few favourites and ignore the rest. Ask whether some new clothes for a favourite doll would go down better. Lego is always a popular choice but it now comes in a range of age levels so make sure that you get the level that fits with the rest of the child's set, as the new pieces will soon be muddled in with the rest.

Lego, Sylvanian Families, Playmobil and other sets with lots of small pieces make great gifts but should be presented at a time when excitement levels are under control. If they are opened on Christmas morning and emptied out on the floor along with everything else, it is unlikely that the full set will ever be reassembled and the lost parts may become a health hazard for younger siblings. Thomas the Tank Engine train sets are wildly popular, but there are several varieties, they are not all compatible with each other, and there is no fun in having more than one of each character. Always check with parents for the precise part/level or set that the child wants.

Bearing gifts

Grandparents who seldom see their grandchildren like to come bearing gifts, and presenting these to the children can certainly be a wonderful icebreaker, especially if the gifts are well chosen. If you are likely to be a more frequent visitor, be careful about starting a tradition you may find burdensome to sustain. The grandchildren will respond to your unconditional love and positive regard even if you come empty-handed, and it is good for them to discover that people love each other for who they are, not what they bring. If you can only visit occasionally and enjoy giving the grandchildren gifts, why not leave it until towards the end? By then you will have an idea what they like and don't already have, and you could even make a memorable outing of buying your 'goodbye present' together.

From time to time you will want to buy the grandchildren things to help you get through a difficult day with them. These are best distinguished from 'presents' by not being wrapped up and by being offered in a low key way, without the expectation of thanks. Puzzles, games and books for a child who is ill or to pass the time on a train journey come into this category. They are best discovered with mild surprise at the bottom of your bag and produced without any fanfare, to avoid a fractious child rejecting them out of sheer contrariness. Because they are not presents, you can take them away with you at the end of the day and bring them out again another time or with another child.

Huang lived far away from their son and his family, but by carefully planning his business trips, Huang was able to make a flying visit, two or three times a year. He always brought a handsome present for Jia Li, his little granddaughter. After a while, Huang's son pointed out that opening and playing with the present absorbed Jia Li for the entire duration of the visit. She was not getting to know her grandfather at all. Huang could not bear to arrive empty-handed, but the next time he came he brought a gift of money for Jia Li. There was no immediate play value in that to distract her, and they struck up a good conversation about what she might spend it on or save up for.

Molly looked after toddler Memphis one day a week in his own home. She had a couple of soft toys and a fire-engine that he loved to play with, so she brought these with her every time she came. Memphis had plenty of toys of his own, but these old friends were always greeted with enthusiasm and provided useful play time while Molly got herself sorted out and settled in.

What not to buy

Child-size versions of adult equipment are no fun unless they actually work. There is not much play value in a toy lawnmower that doesn't cut grass. The same is true for toy musical instruments. Remember that children are technologically savvy these days so a toy version of a smartphone, laptop or i-Pad may light up impressively and play tunes but it will be put aside with contempt by any child much over the age of two unless it has the functionality of the real thing. By the age of four they can probably operate the real versions of these things as well as you can!

Your toybox

You will need toys and games if you are looking after a child in your house. The parents may have some they can give you as many children these days have too much stuff to store comfortably. Otherwise charity shops or ebay are good sources or you could ask for toys as a Christmas or birthday present from your children – a lot more fun than the scarf or tie you might otherwise get. Toy libraries are useful, especially for toddlers, and going to choose toys to borrow makes a bit of an outing. The National Association of Toy and Leisure Libraries will tell you where the nearest one is to you if you email them on helpline@playmatters.co.uk, saying where you live and how old your grandchild is.

It is worth investing in some sort of set with lots of figures to encourage imaginative play, such as a toy farm, zoo, school and so on. If you collect enough of one system to have a couple of settings and a few vehicles to transport the people or animals back and forth between them, the play value shoots up.

Nella remembered how much her own children had enjoyed playing with the old Fisher Price village and circus train. She found she was able to get all the vintage items she remembered, and more, from ebay. As long as she was not bothered about complete sets or items being in boxes, she was able to pick up several job lots quite reasonably. Having already survived some 30 years, and with no electronics to go wrong, the toys proved to be durable enough to survive the attention of her six grandchildren, and she has now stored them in the loft for the next generation.

Try to make sure what you buy for your house is different from the toys the children have at home. If your grandson has a train set at home, go for a basket of cars or an airport at yours. You will certainly need a few dolls/teddies or other soft toys for playing picnic or school. Pop into charity shops when you pass them and see what you can pick up. A toy box can be a bit random to make it more interesting to explore!

A sick grandchild

Whatever childcare you have agreed to do on a regular basis, the chances are that from time to time you will be asked to help out when a child is unwell. Nurseries are rightly insistent that children with fevers, on antibiotics or suffering from diarrhoea are kept at home, and the parents' annual leave can quickly be exhausted if they have to take time off every time their child is ill.

If you are prepared to step in, even at the cost of some of your own annual leave, you will earn the parents' heartfelt thanks and have the satisfaction of being a real support to the family. Your own heart will probably sink at the request, and the worrying will kick in as soon as you agree to do it, but at least you can hand back responsibility at the end of the day.

It helps if you already have a strong bond with the child, so it's worth cementing that relationship when the child is well even if you aren't involved in their regular care. That way, come an emergency, they will see you as a familiar, reliable and well-loved figure, and you will have the advantage of knowing what they are like when they are well.

Most children's illnesses are mild and they recover quickly, so it will usually just be a matter of keeping a fractious child comforted. However, occasionally a child gets seriously ill and then things can develop fast. It is best to be prepared for the worst case scenario even though it is unlikely to happen.

Trust your instincts

Your instincts and experience from your years as a parent will be pretty reliable but the degree of anxiety you feel when the child is not your own is bound to be greater. These days it is easy to keep in touch, so if you are worried, phone or text the parents and share your concerns. On the other hand, you are the adult caring for the child at the time, and if you feel the child is in need of urgent medical attention, trust your instincts and don't hesitate to get it. How you access medical help will depend on where you live and what services are available locally. This will include the child's GP (or yours if the child is staying with you), the ambulance service, out-of-hours and urgent care services and hospital emergency departments. You may need to take a taxi to get there, so it is always a good idea to have cash on you in case of emergencies.

Getting advice

You may be torn between anxiety about the child and guilt at 'bothering' the health services. If you are in two minds about how serious the problem is, NHS Direct provides a very good website that can help you decide **http://www.nhsdirect.nhs.uk/ checksymptoms/topics/children**. You can also call **NHS Direct24** on **0845 4647** for medical advice, 24 hours a day. If they think the child needs to see a GP urgently out of hours they will help arrange this.

Things have changed

You may be surprised at what is recommended by doctors these days. Over the last 20 to 30 years, the way we treat a lot of conditions has changed. Doctors are less likely to prescribe antibiotics, for example, recognising that most infections are viral. Children can overcome these infections naturally and antibiotics don't help.

Sick grandchild checklist

The chances are that you will be looking after a sick child in their home rather than yours. Before the parents leave for work, make sure you have all the information you will need for peace of mind. Get there a bit early so as to have time for a proper briefing and if they have to rush off even so, make sure they phone or text you the answers. You will feel a lot more confident if you know the answers to the questions below. You are not trying to 'play doctor' but you do need to know what to expect and whether something new is developing before your eyes.

■ **In what way is the child ill?**

Fever? Diarrhoea? Cough? Pain? Rash? How long have they had these symptoms? Did anything special seem to trigger the illness? Do they seem to be getting better or worse? Do they have any other conditions you should know about, like eczema or asthma? Have they just had a vaccination? Do they have any allergies? If you do have to speak to a doctor or nurse, you will want these details to hand.

■ **Has professional help been sought?**

Have they already spoken to the doctor, nurse, or baby clinic? If so, what was the advice? Are there any developments they were told to watch out for?

■ **Is the child on medication?**

What should you give and when? Where is it kept? When was the last dose? Is the child likely to refuse it, and if so what strategy do they recommend to get it down? Are they happy for you to give anything else, like ibuprofen or paracetamol, if the child is feverish?

■ **Where is the thermometer kept and how does it work?**

You can probably get an idea if a child is feverish by placing a hand on their forehead, but accurate temperature-taking is much better done scientifically. There are now lots of different kinds of thermometer, and you should find out how their one works before they leave you in charge.

■ **How can the parents be reached?**

Make sure you have a number to call if you are worried. If the child is quite poorly, arranging a planned call at a specific time will be reassuring to you both.

■ **How can medical help be reached?**

Just in case, write down the family doctor's number and make sure you know how to get to the nearest urgent care centre or hospital emergency department.

■ **Any other instructions?**

If there are any detailed instructions, be sure to write them down and carry them out to the letter, to save yourself worrying later whether you did something wrong.

Symptoms and signs

You have of course been through all this before when you were the parent, but illness always seems more alarming in a grandchild. You don't know the child as well as the parents do, so in general be guided by their instructions and their level of concern.

However, with children things can develop fast and you can't count on being able to wait until the parents get back. There are a few situations when you will need to seek medical help directly and without delay. Medical advice is also easier to access during the day than at night.

Fever

Fever is a common feature of childhood illness and means the child's natural defences are kicking in to fight off infection. Fever may occur after vaccinations or when the child is teething. There is no need to call a doctor or to offer medication at home if a child has a fever but seems otherwise well.

You can usually tell when a child is cooking up a high fever because they go pale and shivery and want to lie down. This is a good time to offer medication, in the form of paracetamol or ibuprofen. It doesn't matter too much which one you use, but carefully check the recommended dose for the

child's age. Having both these medications to hand is helpful, as you can alternate them to keep a feverish child comfortable through the day without exceeding the recommended dose of either. Doctors sometimes recommend giving both together to get maximum effect but don't do this without medical instruction. Never give children aspirin, even if it is all you have, as it can make them seriously ill.

Children with fever usually respond to the full age-appropriate dose of medication within an hour or so. If the medication seems to make no difference, that is a cause for concern.

Febrile convulsions

A high fever can sometimes cause a child to have a fit, called a febrile convulsion. These are not uncommon, and not usually serious, but are alarming. The first thing is to make sure the child doesn't hurt himself by banging into table legs or falling off a sofa. If you can position the child on the floor on his side, so much the better. Don't try to force anything between the child's teeth and don't try to restrain the child's movements. Remove any blankets and loosen or remove warm clothing. When the fit is over, and the child has recovered enough to swallow it safely, give the child a dose of paracetamol or ibuprofen to take the temperature down.

If the fit lasts more than a few minutes call 999 to get help. Even if the child recovers quickly, you should still make sure he sees a doctor that day. You will need to find out the cause of the high fever, in case it is something serious like meningitis. The fit itself is unlikely to have any after effects other than a few moments of confusion, and doesn't mean the child has epilepsy. It does mean they may fit again if they get another high fever.

Meningitis

Meningitis isn't common, but it is vitally important to recognise it early. With prompt treatment a child usually recovers fully, but without treatment they may die. The trouble is that it often starts like an ordinary feverish cold and the child doesn't develop the classic signs of a stiff neck or a rash until they are already seriously ill. The rash of meningitis can be distinguished from other childhood rashes by the fact that the spots stay red or purplish even when you press on them. The best way of testing this is to get a glass tumbler and press it firmly on the area. If you can still see red or purple spots through the glass, it could well be meningitis. If the child has dark skin this is harder to be sure about, so look for spots where the skin is lightest. New spots or blotches developing are a sign to get help fast.

A way of testing for stiff neck in a child over 18 months is to ask him to kiss his knees. However, most under-fives with meningitis don't get a stiff neck, so this test doesn't rule it out.

If a child with a fever does get a rash that doesn't blanch on pressure or has a stiff neck you must get professional help immediately. Call an ambulance or take the child to the hospital emergency department, contacting the parents as soon as you can.

Even in the absence of a stiff neck or rash, any child who seems more ill than you would expect from a feverish cold, and doesn't respond to paracetamol or ibuprofen, should give you cause for concern. Worrying signs and symptoms are cold hands and feet, limb pains, skin that looks pale or blotchy, vomiting, a cry that sounds different, rapid breathing, irritability, floppiness, or unresponsiveness. Trust your instincts. Call the doctor, mentioning your anxiety about meningitis, or get the child straight to the hospital emergency department, contacting the parents as soon as you can. Meningitis in young children progresses very quickly. You can't afford just to wait for the parents to come home.

Anyone looking after children needs to be familiar with the signs and symptoms of meningitis. The NHS Choices website has a useful illustrated list that you can print out and stick on your memo board or keep in your wallet. **http://www.nhs.uk/Tools/Documents/Meningitis%20symptoms.pdf.**

The Meningitis Trust has an excellent website **http://www.meningitis-trust.org/meningitis-info/signs-and-symptoms/babies-and-toddlers/** detailing all the possible signs and symptoms.

Cough

Children seem to spend their first few years with a constantly runny nose and recurrent cough, especially if they have lots of contact with other children at nursery or playgroup. These upper respiratory infections are usually viral, mild and important for developing immunity. If the children don't get exposed to these bugs now, they will catch them later when they start school. A cause for concern is if the child seems to be having trouble breathing, or if they look blue around the mouth or finger tips. Call the doctor or take the child to an urgent care centre or hospital emergency department, contacting the parents as soon as you can.

Delerium or confusion

A child who has hallucinations or talks in a confused rambling way is a cause for concern. Meningitis or pneumonia can cause this behaviour and the child needs urgent treatment. Confusion after a head injury is also a serious sign. Call the doctor or take the child to an urgent care centre or hospital emergency department, contacting the parents as soon as you can.

Headache

Fever and headaches often come and go together, but a headache is a worrying symptom if the child has had a recent head injury or if she complains of not being able to see properly or is acting peculiarly. Call the doctor or take the child to an urgent care centre or hospital emergency department, contacting the parents as soon as you can.

An informative website with information about headache and associated symptoms is **www.headsmart.org.uk**.

Lethargy

It is normal for a child who isn't well to sleep more during the day, or to want to sit on your lap and be cuddled, but if they are difficult to rouse, or seem floppy, that is a cause for concern. Call the doctor or take the child to an urgent care centre or hospital emergency department, contacting the parents as soon as you can.

Things move fast with children. They can get worse suddenly, even after being checked over by a doctor or nurse and pronounced fine. Don't be afraid to go back or to take the child to the emergency department if your instincts tell you the child is not right.

When Laura came to look after Chloe on the fourth day of the illness she was alarmed to find the baby still feverish, covered all over in angry looking spots, lethargic and floppy. Laura was not happy and called Chloe's mother at work, offering to take her to the doctor. The mother said she had taken the child to the doctor the day before and had been told not to worry, the baby would be fine. Laura's instinct was that the child had deteriorated since then, so she held her ground. This time the doctor said that the spots had become infected and Chloe was admitted to hospital.

Diarrhoea and vomiting

Occasional episodes of vomiting or loose stools are common in children, and usually get better with time and plenty of fluids. Sometimes children pick up gastrointestinal infections, and that can be more serious, especially if they become dehydrated. A child with diarrhoea may become dehydrated even if they are drinking the usual amount. Encourage frequent drinks, giving a baby their usual amount of milk plus extra fluids in between feeds, in the form of rehydration fluids from the chemist, as advised by the baby's doctor.

With older children, offer diluted apple juice, and other diluted sweet drinks. Salty snacks such as crisps may be welcomed and help replenish salt loss. Keep an eye on how much they are urinating.

Get urgent medical advice if the child looks ill, has a dry nappy or no desire to urinate for several hours, has persistent tummy pain, vomits repeatedly or passes several watery stools in the course of a day.

Earache

Ear infections are common. The child may have a red outer ear or rub her ear and cry distressfully. Most earache is related to viral infections and settles in one or two days with paracetamol or ibuprofen. It is the pressure on the eardrum rather than the infection itself that causes the pain. If earache persists beyond two days or there is any discharge the ear should be looked at by a doctor, as some will need an antibiotic.

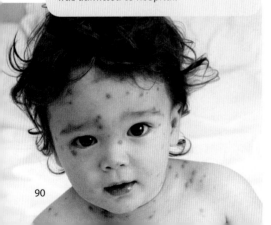

Caring for a sick child

Medication

Some children enjoy taking medicine, but most don't. These days the medicines often come with small syringes rather than spoons, or you can ask the pharmacist or doctor for one. They are great for accurate measurement of the doses and for squirting the medicine into the child's mouth. Aim for the inside of the cheek rather than the back of the throat to avoid setting off a gag reflex. Some toddlers like to hold the syringe and squirt it in themselves. Mixing medicine with yoghurt, ice cream or a spoonful of jam can work, as long as you get the full dose down.

Feeding

In general, sick children lose their appetites and it is best not to try to get food into them, as they don't need it and they may just vomit it all back up and feel worse. Focus on keeping them hydrated. With babies under a year, milk is what they digest best and has the best balance of nutrients for them. A baby who refuses two feeds in a row is a cause for concern and you should get advice from the parents or the doctor.

Older children with diarrhoea are best off drinking clear fluids and not eating anything much until their tummies settle down and they feel like it. Milk and high fibre foods are best avoided.

When the child starts eating again, little and often is the best strategy. Grapes, banana slices, berries, toast, crackers, ice cream or ice lollies work pretty well. Offer them in small quantities at regular intervals throughout the day, and take them away without fuss if uneaten.

Keeping a sick child entertained

A child who is too sick to go to playgroup or nursery but is well enough to be bored staying at home can be demanding. This is when television or DVDs can be a godsend. Normal rules about screen hours can be relaxed when children are ill, and with any luck they will fall asleep on the sofa.

Board or card games, sticker books, paper dolls and arts and crafts can all help to while away the time. Children become a bit more babyish when they are sick so familiar DVDs and books, and easy puzzles work better than the next age group up in a complex construction model.

In conclusion

Looking after a sick grandchild is bound to be a worry and a responsibility, but it isn't usually all that bad. Children get lots of minor ailments and usually bounce back as quickly as they get sick. The chances of them getting seriously ill on your watch are small. Should this happen, doctors and nurses are attuned to the fact that children can deteriorate very quickly and you are unlikely to be criticised for seeking help, or for coming back if things don't go as predicted. The good news is that even among children who look sick enough to be admitted to hospital, the majority are discharged within 12 hours, either on treatment or having got better without any.

For more information about signs and symptoms in sick children, this website is useful: **www.nhsdirect.nhs.uk/en/CheckSymptoms/Topics/Children**

Accidents and emergencies

Serious accidents and emergencies are not likely to happen to your grandchild while you are caring for them, but they can happen and you should know what to do. Staying calm and taking prompt and correct action can save your grandchild's life.

You should know how to get help in an emergency situation. If you are not already sure where the nearest emergency department or urgent care centre is, or what the phone number of the child's GP is, get hold of this information and keep it where you can find it in an emergency.

First aid kit

You should keep a first aid kit in the house, stored where you can easily find it. These can be bought quite reasonably from a range of suppliers. Look for one that is suitable for children and for home use. Kits designed for childminders or schools will have more supplies in them than you are likely to need. Alternatively, you can use a box of your own and purchase the contents at the chemist. The minimum you will need to include are:

Cold running water straight from the tap is the best way of cleaning a wound.

If you take the children out in the car, keep a first-aid kit in the boot too, and make sure you always have a bottle of drinking water available for offering a drink to a shocked child and for washing out wounds or scrapes if there is no tap nearby.

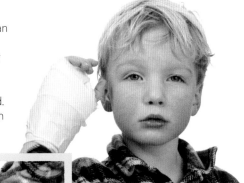

+ one box of children's plasters - for minor cuts and grazes

+ one pair of sterile gloves - in case your hands are dirty or the injury is bloody

+ three packs of sterile low adherent dressings in different sizes – for different sized injuries

+ one roll of gauze bandaging – to keep the dressing in place

+ one roll of micropore tape - for securing the bandaging

+ two sterile eyepads - for covering an injured eye en route to seeking medical attention

+ one triangular bandage with two safety pins - for making a sling for an injured arm

+ one pair of tough blunt-ended scissors - for cutting clothes

+ one pair of tweezers – for pulling out splinters or thorns

Cuts and bruises

If you never hand your grandchild back at the end of the day a little bit bumped or bruised, you probably aren't getting her out enough. The odd grazed knee or elbow is just part of growing up.

To treat a minor cut or graze, wash the wound in running water to get any dirt out. An optional smear of antiseptic cream and perhaps a sterile plaster (provided your grandchild is not allergic to plasters) and all should be well. It is worth having a variety of children's plasters for the purpose. Choosing which one to have is a useful distraction for a tearful child.

To treat a cut lip, press on it gently with a clean cold wet cloth (a clean wet handkerchief with an ice cube in it is good) until the bleeding stops. Don't offer the child anything acid or spicy to eat or drink until it has closed over as it will make the cut sting. If the cut extends beyond the vermilion border it may leave a scar so get the child to an emergency department.

A bag of frozen peas makes a good ice-pack for bumps and bruises. Grabbing one is quicker than emptying an ice tray and the bag is more malleable. Wrap the bag of peas in a tea-towel first and don't leave it on for more than a few minutes.

Any cut that is big, deep, gaping or seems to have anything in it like bits of dirt or glass, or won't stop bleeding, needs immediate medical attention.

Falls

If a child has fallen from a height, first check for obvious injury or bleeding, and for consciousness. Usually there will be a few moments of heart-stopping silence followed by crying. Talk to him, soothe him and try to assess the situation calmly. Hold an icepack, if available, to any lump that is forming. Follow your instincts, and if you feel something is not right, get medical advice. If the child does any of the following, call an ambulance or get him to the nearest emergency department yourself:

- stops breathing or is struggling for breath
- is unconscious even briefly or seems unaware of what's going on
- has a fit
- can't use a limb
- vomits repeatedly
- looks unwell.

Burns and scalds

If your grandchild is burned or scalded, first remove her and yourself from further danger and then assess the extent of the injury. If the skin is red but not mottled or blistered and the damage is not extensive, hold the burnt area under a cold running tap for a few minutes. Or cool it by wetting a clean tea towel and laying it on the area. Don't apply ice which may damage the skin further and don't let the child get chilled. Don't put butter or any other kind of cream or ointment on the burn. Assess whether you need to seek medical help. If you find any of the following, call an ambulance or get her to the nearest emergency department yourself:

- the affected area is extensive
- skin looks mottled, raw or blistered
- clothing is sticking to the skin
- the child is looking shocked.

Pills and poisons

If your grandchild has found your medications and may have swallowed some, first have a quick search around for any tablets that may have fallen on the floor and rolled away and then see if you can quickly work out how many have been taken. If it is just one or two, call the doctor or emergency service for advice. If she could have swallowed more, then get the child straight to an emergency department. Don't try to make her sick and don't wait and see. Take the bottle or pack with you so that the doctor knows exactly what medication was taken.

Household cleaners, dishwasher tablets, washing-machine liquid capsules and garden chemicals are all highly toxic and often corrosive too, so get the child to an emergency department straight away if they have been exposed to these dangerous substances.

Choking

If something goes down the 'wrong way', the child's natural reaction is to cough to expel it. If she is coughing and spluttering, just calm her down and encourage her to cough. Don't apply first-aid techniques to a child who can speak, cough and breathe. You could make matters worse.

If she can't cough or talk and is struggling to breathe or looking blue, you will have to take immediate action. If anyone else is in earshot shout at them to call an ambulance at once, otherwise do so yourself, but not before making a determined attempt to dislodge the obstruction. Stay calm. Don't poke or sweep blindly in the mouth, as you may push the obstruction further down. Look in her mouth. If you can see and grip the obstruction, for instance one end of a piece of popped balloon or a strip of meat, then extract it.

To dislodge an obstruction that you can't see and pull out you need a combination of gravity and sudden air pressure coming from the lungs. Lie a baby head down along your forearm, or small child across your lap, or get a larger child to sit or stand leaning forward, head down. Tip the child's chin up slightly with one hand and deliver five sharp thumps on the back with your other hand, between the shoulder blades. Check for success after each thump. If that doesn't work, give five abdominal thrusts. Several attempts are usually needed for success so don't give up after just one or two goes.

These procedures are easier to understand by demonstration than by reading about them. There is a video on **http://www.redcross.org.uk/What-we-do/First-aid/Children-First-Aid/Choking-child**, and another on **http://on.aol.com/video/how-to-deal-with-a-choking-baby-118122835**. Better still is to go on a paediatric first aid course that lets you practise on dummy, under supervision.

When life gets tough

Sad things happen in life, and when they happen to families, grandparents can make an important difference. Having a loving relationship with a grandparent can buffer a child against the impact of traumatic childhood experiences.

Oliver was three when his father walked out on them. His mother had to go back to work so his grandmother Jennifer took on his care three days a week. Oliver was very difficult, kicking, biting, screaming and swearing. Jennifer listened to him patiently and showed him a room he could go in when he felt frustrated or angry. Gradually he calmed down. Her daughter had instructed Jennifer not to tell Oliver why his father had disappeared so suddenly, but every now and then Oliver would burst out tearfully with, 'Why doesn't Dad love me?' Jennifer didn't know what to say except, 'Grandma loves you sweetheart, and always will.' That seemed to comfort him.

In general, grandparents can choose whether or not to get involved in the care of their grandchildren, but there are times when we realise we have to step up to the plate, however much it upsets our own plans. When we were researching this book we heard moving stories about grandparents who stepped in to do everything from providing day care for a disabled grandchild to taking their grandchildren into their home and raising them.

Special needs and disabilities

Serious developmental problems are usually picked up during one of the regular developmental checks at birth, one and two years of age. Less severe or later-developing problems may not become clear until starting school. Whoever spends most time looking after a child is the most likely person to spot the problem first. Usually this will be the parents, but if you are taking on major childcare responsibilities, it may be you. While it is not a good idea to spend a lot of time comparing your grandchild's progress to milestones on development charts, it is your responsibility to share any concerns you may have with the parents, having done what you can to ensure that you are not over-reacting.

Robbie was a late talker. He was obsessed with his toy trains, even holding them while he ate. He seemed dreamy and in his own world. His grandparents put this down to the fact that his parents had split up. By the time he was three they started to worry about the obsessive way he lined up his cars, over and over, and the fact that almost everything he said still seemed to be a repetition of what they had just said to him. They raised their concerns with his mother, who agreed to take him to see his GP. By the time Robbie started school he had been diagnosed as autistic and was lined up to get the extra help he would need.

Linda has a six-year old boy with significant learning disabilities. She said, 'The most important thing a grandparent can do is accept the child for who they are and be their champion. My dad right from the word go has always been Alex's number one fan and loves him for being Alex – seeing through any label or diagnosis or difficulty and it's always meant the world to me.'

There are some websites with useful information about developmental milestones that may help you decide whether you are right to think there is a problem:

- www.direct.gov.uk/en/Parents/ Schoolslearninganddevelopment/ SpecialEducationalNeeds/index.htm

- www.education.gov.uk/publications/standard publicationDetail/Page1/DFE-00046-2012

- www.healthvisitors.com/parents/ development_two_yrs.htm

The two most important things you can offer a child with any kind of disability are time and love. Focus on the child's individual qualities, appreciate his efforts, praise his achievements and recognise his abilities. Compare him to where he was rather than where other children are at his age. Give him plenty of time to practise his skills and be someone with whom it is always safe to try and fail without being given up on.

You may be able to play a part in directly caring for the child, learning how to meet his needs so as to be able to give the parents a break. Or you may help more by looking after his siblings and making sure they get to do the things their parents don't have time to do with them.

You may be able to help by writing some of the letters and making some of the calls that the parents seem to have to make to get all the support they need from the system. Parents of children with disabilities whose grandparents are closely involved in their care also get more support from other sources.

> Melissa said, 'My mother helped by supporting me through my shock and upset with Charlie and by looking after him and being smiley and happy when I was finding it difficult to be positive! Parents somehow manage to do the practical tasks but find it hard to be all smiley and up beat all the time. Grandparents can provide this, as well as more babysitting than usual so the parents can get out a bit and have time for themselves.'

There is useful information about grandparenting a disabled child on this website: **www.grandparents-association. org.uk/childcare/are-you-looking-after-a-disabled-grandchild-during-the-week.html**

Taking on the role of parents

In the US it is estimated that 11% of children are being raised by a 'parenting grandparent'. The reasons for this include parental death or illness, marital breakup, alcohol or substance misuse and imprisonment. There is no question that taking on the role of parents is hard on the grandparents, whose own plans and way of life are sacrificed in the process, but it is a responsibility most of us would accept rather than have our grandchildren cared for by strangers. If you are in this situation there is support and information available on the website **www. grandparentsasparents.org.uk**

> Gwen was shocked when her daughter-in-law was diagnosed as an alcoholic. Her son told her of disturbing instances like the time his wife was so drunk that she forgot to pick up the twins from the childminder. There were instances of his wife driving while under the influence of alcohol. Social services became involved and her son turned to Gwen in desperation. Gwen felt she had no choice but to put her retirement plans on hold and take over the care of the children while her son looked after his wife.

When parents split up

If the parents split up, you may need to work at maintaining contact with your grandchildren, especially if it is not your own child who has custody. It may be tempting to express your disapproval of the behaviour of the parents by withdrawing your support, but focus on the needs of your grandchildren. This may be the very time when you could make a real difference to them, perhaps by providing a temporary home, or a base for visits with the parent who has left them. The children may want to talk about what happened, and the rule has to be, no criticising, no blaming, no hostility. No matter how you feel, treat both parents and any new partners they may present to you with unfailing respect and courtesy. Your relationship with your grandchildren takes precedence over your feelings about their parents' behaviour.

Losing contact

As a rule, grandparents do not occupy the centre stage in a family. Some families speak of formidable grandparents who reign over the family by controlling its wealth, but that set-up is not common. Mostly grandparents trust their offspring to take responsibility for their own families and recognise that they have become minor players, nice to have but dispensable. The law seems to take the same view. Grandparents do not have any automatic right of access to their grandchildren and when parents move away, split up, or when one parent dies, they can lose contact.

You can apply for access to your grandchildren through a contact order, but as a grandparent you have to get permission from a court first, before you are allowed to apply. To be successful you then have to prove more than your kinship. You have to convince a court that you present no threat to the child or to family relationships and that you have a significant relationship with the child that is of benefit to him. If you are in this situation, you will need expert advice from a lawyer experienced in family law. If things have got to this state it is unlikely that you will be able to do much more than keep in touch from a distance, but even that is worth doing, to show that your love for your grandchild is undiminished by the separation and that he will always be a very special person to you.

Marian and Derek were devastated when their son was killed in a car accident. They supported their daughter-in-law as best they could by looking after their little grandson while she went back to work, and gained comfort from having the toddler around. It was like a second bereavement when their daughter-in-law told them she had met someone else, and would be moving away to live with him and start a new life. That was the last time they saw either her or the grandson they had become so fond of.

Death in the family

Talking to friends and relatives about their own grandparents, we were struck by how the role of the grandparent changed when a parent or child died. In many cases, the grandparent became the source of invaluable support to the grieving family. The grandparent was a calm, reliable, loving presence who was willing to talk about what had happened and how the child felt about it. Practical help was important too, especially

When Caroline's little brother died her mother became withdrawn and her father, unable to cope, left home. Caroline's grandmother was overwhelmed with grief and stopped visiting. Caroline was left feeling abandoned, unloved and guilty to have been the child to survive. The effect of the tragedy on her was profound and long-lasting.

When Abby's father died, she was ten. Her grandfather took to visiting the family every Saturday. He brought his toolbox and fixed anything that needed fixing and then took her mother to the supermarket to do a big shop. After the chores were done he would stay for the rest of the day, reading the paper, watching television, and just being there. 'He was so reliable, like a rod,' Abby remembered. 'You could talk to him about anything, and he always knew what you should do.'

when it was one of the parents who had died. Grandparents stepping in to fill at least a part of the role of the lost parent made a huge difference to the family and softened the impact of the bereavement on the child.

Sadly, we also heard several stories of how the overwhelming grief of grandparents led them to withdraw, unable to cope, just at the time when they could have been such a support to their grandchildren.

Looking after yourself

You need to look after yourself if you want to look after the grandchildren. The rewards are huge, and well worth every pain, but it would be folly to pretend it is all fun and games.

It would be wrong to deny the financial, physical and mental strain that looking after small children involves. Looking after children is tiring, and they share their continual virus infections with you. The cries of babies are a strain on the nerves and carrying them about is a strain on the back. A tantruming toddler or a whining pre-schooler will try the patience of a saint. You worry about keeping them safe and happy and under control, about your relationship with the parents, and about the impact childcare is having on your job, and your other significant relationships.

None of these are arguments against doing it, just against taking on more than you can cope with and in favour of doing everything you can to keep healthy and manage the stress.

Stressbusters

1 Take regular exercise

Don't assume that carrying a baby around, going shopping with a toddler, or clearing up the mess a pre-schooler's arts and crafts session makes is enough to keep you fit. It is exhausting and you need to be fit to do it, but it isn't the kind of exercise that gets you in shape. You need at least 45 minutes of vigorous exercise three times a week, enough to make you puff at least some of the time. You can get some of your exercise while looking after the child – going for a good long fast-paced walk with the pushchair would do it. Or you can get a workout playing ball or hide and seek with children – but you have to do your share of the running around. There is an NHS website with a lot of great ideas for getting fit for free: **www.nhs.uk/ Livewell/fitness/Pages/free-fitness. aspx**

2 Eat properly

If you are too tired to make a proper meal at the end of a childcare day, have your main meal with the child. You should be providing something nutritious and balanced for her anyway, and eating together is a social occasion. Don't even think about finishing what she leaves on her plate though! You will take in quite enough of her viruses without doing this, and the extra calories may be hard to work off.

Get an annual flu jab

It is not so much that you don't want to give her the flu as that she may give it to you.

Get enough rest

If you are helping out overnight by looking after babies or children who wake you in the small hours, remember that the older you are the harder it is to cope with sleep deprivation. Factor in your need for a nap or an undisturbed night to follow.

Develop your support system

Rope in the child's other grandparents and discuss how you can share the load and cover for each other. Join the Grandparents' Association **www. grandparents-association.org.uk/** which has a web forum and lots of information, including whether there is a grandparents and toddlers group near you.

Get a life

Or hang on to the one you already have. Make sure you don't let caring for your grandchildren crowd out all your other interests. It won't be long before the toddler is off to school and you don't want to find you have lost your circle of friends in the interim. You will have more to offer your grandchildren if you maintain a range of interests and activities.

7) Don't take risks

Reduce your worry by taking all reasonable steps to make sure your grandchildren will be safe in your charge, wherever you are looking after them.

8) Don't take on too much

No one gains if you make yourself ill through exhaustion. Recognise that your capacity to heave small children about decreases with age, as does your ability to run after two or three at the same time. Don't stretch yourself to the limit with regular commitments. Leave some reserves in the tank for emergencies.

9) Reduce uncertainty

Uncertainty is unsettling. Once a year have a full and frank talk with the parents about what is likely to change in the year ahead. Have a conversation with them about the changes, making sure it is clear what you will and will not be doing.

10) Make time for holidays

Everyone needs a childfree break from time to time!

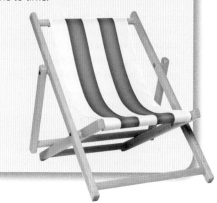

Friends to the end

The lovely thing about putting time in when the grandchildren are little is that you establish a firm friendship that can last for many years. Even when they are old enough not to need 'looking after' they will want to visit you and tell you things.

As a teenager, Christiana's grandaughter used to drop in after school at least once a week with two or three friends, 'just to talk about things and hang out.' Christiana loved to listen to their stories of friendships and feuds and they were interested in her psychological insights.

Sanjiv had always been close to his grandfather and recalls visiting him during the university holidays. The elderly man was coming to the end of his years, and enjoyed being visited. 'It wasn't an act of charity, I got a lot of wisdom from him. He was a very worldly man.'

Death of a grandparent

For most children, the loss of a grandparent is their first experience of bereavement, and it can be very upsetting. The stronger the bond between you and your grandchildren, the more it will affect them when your time, or that of your spouse comes. Considering this from the child's perspective, there are steps you can take to make this experience less traumatic.

The Tavistock and Portman NHS Trust has produced a very useful booklet about how to support a child when a grandparent dies. **www.tavistockandportman.nhs.uk/sites/default/files/Coping%20with%20the%20death%20of%20a%20grandparent.pdf**

People in every culture have developed ceremonies and rituals around death. Whatever the custom or ceremony, it helps to bring the grieving to a climax and a close. Children need closure as much as adults. Obviously, it will be up to the parents to decide how to involve the children, but offering them a role in the ceremony acknowledges that very special bond they had with the grandparent who has died.

When Angela's husband died at home, her children were gathered in her house, along with several grandchildren. Angela smoothed the bedcovers, tidied the bedroom, brought up flowers and lit some candles. Then she invited the grandchildren up one by one to say goodbye to their grandfather if they wanted. They all did. After that, she sat the family round to plan how each of her children and grandchildren would have a special role to play in the funeral service. Once that was done, she was able to do her own grieving.

Talking about death

Death is one of the great taboos in our society. People hate talking about it, especially to children, and often use confusing euphemisms. Another source of confusion for children in a multi-cultural society is the range of views they are likely to encounter about what happens after death. You may find your views being canvassed by a child trying to make sense of it all, so talk to the parents about how they want you to deal with these questions. It is not your job to impose your views but you may find the parents are happy for you to share your beliefs with the child. If not, then don't.

Ben and Ella, aged three and five, became interested in death when their great-grandmother died. They didn't know her very well and handled her departure with perfect equanimity, but they started asking their grandmother Kathy questions about what it meant to die, and when was that likely to happen to her. So Kathy explained about being born and growing up and getting old and dying as the cycle of life. 'It's like a story,' she said. 'There is a beginning, a middle and an end. Stories need an ending. I haven't got to my ending yet, I am having my happy ever afters!' And swept them into a big hug.

Saying a good good-bye

The stronger the bond you have developed with your grandchildren, the more you will want to help them cope with your death when it comes.

When Helena's mother died suddenly, her grandchildren found it hard to believe that she would just go, without saying goodbye. Remembering that, Helena started a 'memory folder' for each of her own grandchildren, slipping in tickets, programmes, photos and other mementoes of days together. She added any cards or notes they sent her, and pictures they had drawn for her. On her birthday each year she added a little note to each folder about what she thought about their achievements and how proud she was of them as they were growing up. She hasn't shown the folders to the grandchildren because she wants them to be a surprise, her way of telling them how much she loved them and why, one last time.

Think about your relationship with each of the grandchildren and what it is that they might get comfort from in the event of your death. When our mother died at 98, having suffered from dementia for the final years of her life, we found an envelope in her desk marked, 'To be opened in the event of my death.' Inside was a letter she had written to us ten years previously when she still had all her faculties. It told us not to grieve, how her love would always be with us, and ended with a special message for each of us about what she admired and loved about us. To hear that beloved strong voice one more time, beyond all expectation, was most wonderfully comforting. We each resolved to do the same, for our children and our grandchildren.

It is one of the great privileges of living as long as many people do these days, that you can watch your grandchildren grow up, and even look forward to making the acquaintance of their own children in time. The personal sacrifices, hard work and expense of caring for the grandchildren when they are small seem a small price to pay for a friendship that can last the rest of your life.

We found the following resources useful - but we cannot vouch for the accuracy of everything on these websites.

For information about grandparenting:

www.grannynet.co.uk

www.grandparentsasparents.org.uk

www.grandparents-association.org.uk

To find out your nearest toy library:

Email helpline@playmatters.co.uk

For information about childcare:

www.daycaretrust.org.uk

For information about pets and safety:

http://www.doggonesafe.com/baby_safety_around_dogs

http://www.safekids.co.uk/catsandbabiesorchildren.html

For more safety tips:

www.safekids.co.uk/AroundtheHomeCategory.html

www.rospa.com/childsafety

www.rospa.com/leisuresafety/adviceandinformation/leisuresafety/trampoline-safety.aspx

http://www.poison.vcu.edu/pdfs/art_products.pdf

http://www.littlehelper.co.uk

For leisure ideas:

http://toolserver.org/~stephankn/playground

http://www.nationaltrust.org.uk

For reading about sickness or accidents in children:

http://www.meningitis-trust.org/meningitis-info/signs-and-symptoms/babies-and-toddlers/

www.nhsdirect.nhs.uk/en/CheckSymptoms/Topics/Children

http://www.nhs.uk/Tools/Documents/Meningitis%20symptoms.pdf

www.headsmart.org.uk/

http://www.redcross.org.uk/What-we-do/First-aid/Children-First-Aid/Choking-child

http://on.aol.com/video/how-to-deal-with-a-choking-baby-118122835

For information about education and development:

www.direct.gov.uk/en/Parents/Schoolslearninganddevelopment/SpecialEducationalNeeds/index.htm

www.education.gov.uk/publications/standard/publicationDetail/Page1/DFE-00046-2012

www.healthvisitors.com/parents/development_two_yrs.htm

For ideas to keep fit:

www.nhs.uk/Livewell/fitness/Pages/free-fitness.aspx

For helping a child after the death of a grandparent

www.tavistockandportman.nhs.uk/sites/default/files/Coping%20with%20the%20death%20of%20a%20grandparent.pdf

---

Some books we found useful

Baby to Toddler Month By Month. Simone Cave, Dr. Caroline Fertleman. 2011, Hay House UK

Coping with Two: A Stress-free Guide to Managing a New Baby When You Have Another Child. Simone Cave, Dr. Caroline Fertleman. 2012, Hay House, UK

How to raise an amazing child the Montessori way. Tim Seldin. 2006. DK Publishing

Small Steps Forward: Using Games and Activities to Help Your Pre-school Child with Special Needs. Sarah Newman, Jeanie Mellersh. 2008. Jessica Kingsley Publishers UK.

The Great Ormond Street New Baby & Child Care Book: The Essential Guide for Parents of Children Aged 0-5. Maire Messenger, Tessa Hilton. Revised edition, 2004. Vermilion, Ebury Press, Random house UK.

Your Baby Week By Week: The ultimate guide to caring for your new baby by Dr Caroline Fertleman and Simone Cave. 2007, Vermilion, Ebury Press, Random House UK.